What I Believe

What I Believe

Tariq Ramadan

OXFORD
UNIVERSITY PRESS

2010

OXFORD
UNIVERSITY PRESS

Oxford University Press, Inc., publishes works that further
Oxford University's objective of excellence
in research, scholarship, and education.

Oxford   New York

Auckland   Cape Town   Dar es Salaam   Hong Kong   Karachi
Kuala Lumpur   Madrid   Melbourne   Mexico City   Nairobi
New Delhi   Shanghai   Taipei   Toronto

With offices in

Argentina   Austria   Brazil   Chile   Czech Republic   France   Greece
Guatemala   Hungary   Italy   Japan   Poland   Portugal   Singapore
South Korea   Switzerland   Thailand   Turkey   Ukraine   Vietnam

Published in Italian as *Islam e libertà*

Published by Oxford University Press, Inc.
198 Madison Avenue, New York, NY 10016

www.oup.com

Oxford is a registered trademark of Oxford University Press

Library of Congress Cataloging-in-Publication Data
Ramadan, Tariq.
What I believe / Tariq Ramadan.
p. cm.
Includes bibliographical references and index.
ISBN 978-0-19-538785-8
1. Ramadan, Tariq. 2. Scholars, Muslim—Biography.
3. Islam—21st century. 4. East and West. I. Title.
BP80.R343A3   2010
297.2—DC22   2009015320

1 3 5 7 9 8 6 4 2
Printed in the United States of America
on acid-free paper

To Diana Eck,

Cynthia Read,

Jameel Jaffer,

John Esposito,

Peter Mandaville

Contents

Acknowledgments

This book would not have been written without the insistence of Andrea Romano, who pressed me to write a short text presenting the substance of my thought beyond controversy and polemics. I am grateful for his proposal and insistence. There are so many women and men I should thank here for their love, their friendship, and their presence, as well as their constructive criticism. Whether in the Muslim majority countries of the Middle East, Asia, and Africa or in the Muslim communities of Canada, the United States, Australia, New Zealand, Mauritius, South Africa, and Europe; I have learned so much from `ulamâ, intellectuals, leaders, and organization managers, as well as ordinary, anonymous, sincere, devoted women and men. Books can never replace human beings: I thank each of you, without naming anyone so that no one is forgotten, for your presence and for your gifts, so important and so different in nature.

I have learned so much in the West, from my training, my readings, my commitment, and, above all, so many encounters. Here again, it would be impossible to express my gratitude nominally. But let me simply recall a few first names, who may recognize themselves: Alain, Catherine, Cynthia, Diana, Dick, François, Françoise, Han, Jameel, Jean, Joellyn, John, Marjolein, Melissa, Michel, Monique, Peter, Pierre, Richard...there are so many others.

In Switzerland, in Geneva, there is a mother who loves and who prays. Her presence is light and protection. There is also a large family, brothers, a sister, nieces and nephews. Najma, Moussa, Sami, Maryam, and Iman, always. My heart loves you and thanks you.

London, June 2009

What I Believe

Introduction

THIS BOOK IS A WORK OF CLARIFICATION, a deliberately accessible presentation of the basic ideas I have been defending for more than twenty years. It is intended for those who have little time to spare: ordinary citizens, politicians, journalists, perhaps some social workers or teachers who may be in a bit of a hurry but who want to understand and possibly to check things out. Rather than entering my name in a web search engine (and coming up with the million links that mainly report what others have written about me) or being content with the so-called free virtual encyclopedias that are in fact so biased (like Wikipedia, where the factual errors and partisan readings are astounding), I give readers this opportunity to read me in the original and simply get direct access to my thought.

In recent years I have been presented as a "controversial intellectual." What this means is not quite clear, but in effect everyone admits that a controversial intellectual is one whose thought does not leave people indifferent: some praise it, others criticize it, but in any case it causes them to react and think. I have never kept to a single field of intervention: I have not dealt only with the "Islamic religion," although it is important to note that one of the areas I work on is indeed theological and legal reflection starting from within Islamic references. I do not represent all Muslims but I belong to the reformist trend. I aim to remain faithful to the principles of Islam, on the basis of scriptural sources, while taking into account the evolution of historical and geographical contexts. Many readers who have not yet looked into religious issues or who have limited knowledge of the subject sometimes find it difficult to understand my approach and methodology. Unlike literalists who merely rely on quoting verses, reformists must take the time to put things in perspective, to contextualize, and to suggest new understandings. To grasp this reasoning, readers or listeners must follow it from beginning to end: if they do not they may misunderstand its conclusions and consider that there are contradictions or that it involves "doublespeak." Things should be clarified: doublespeak consists in saying one thing in front of an audience to flatter or mislead them, and something else, different in content, elsewhere, to a different audience or in a different language. Adapting one's level of speech to one's audience, or adapting the nature of one's references, is not doublespeak. When addressing my students I use elevated language with philosophical references that they can understand; when speaking before social protagonists or manual laborers, I also use appropriate speech and illustrations; and if I speak to Muslims, my language and references also take into account their level of discourse and their universe of understanding. This is a necessary pedagogy. To avoid doublespeak, what matters is that the substance of the discourse does not change.

Regarding Islamic references, my approach has constantly been to develop themes in three distinct steps. First, I quote the sources: here is a verse or a Prophetic tradition (*hadîth*) and this is the literal meaning. Second, I explain the different readings offered by scholars in the course of history as well as the possibilities available for interpreting the said verse or *hadîth*, because of its formulation or in light of Islam's message. Third, starting from the verse (or *hadîth*) and its various possible interpretations, I suggest an understanding and implementation that take into account the context in which we live. That is what I call the reformist approach.

For example: (1) There are indeed texts (one verse, and hence some Prophetic traditions) that refer to striking one's wife: I quote them because Muslims read and quote those texts. (2) Here are the interpretations that have been suggested, from the most literalist, which justify striking women in the name of the Quran, to the most reformist, which read this verse in light of the global message and contextualize the verse and Prophetic traditions as well as taking their chronology into account. (3) In light of those interpretations and considering the example set by the Prophet, who never struck a woman, I say that domestic violence contradicts Islamic teachings and that such behavior must be condemned.

If my readers or listeners stop at the first step in my development (or if a reviewer, willfully or not, quotes only part of it), they cut short my reasoning; they may even claim that I say the same as the literalists and accuse me of doublespeak. Of course I quote the same verses as the literalists, but my conclusions are different! And it is because I systematically start from the sources and their interpretation that Muslims listen to my lectures, read my books, and relate to them.

I have also focused on philosophical, social, cultural, and political issues (at both national and international levels). All those fields of study are of course linked in one way or another, but I have always been careful not to confuse orders. Because of the confusion I observe in contemporary debates about societal issues (identities, religions, cultures, insecurity, immigration, marginalization, and so on), I have attempted to deconstruct and classify problems, though without disconnecting them. I hope the present work will confirm this commitment and this approach and methodology.

As mentioned above, some people have claimed that I used doublespeak without ever providing clear evidence. A rumor has been fostered and journalists repeat it: "He is reported to use doublespeak, and so on." This is easy criticism: it is often the unverifiable (and unverified) argument of those who have no argument and have verified nothing. It is also frequently a clever reversal performed by those who, deliberately or not, have a "double hearing" and hear very selectively. I will not waste my time here trying to defend myself: I have no desire or time for this. It is nonetheless important for the reader to understand why what I say can give rise to such passion and reactions. I know that I disturb and I know whom I disturb. When speaking about religion, philosophy, or politics, I have necessarily, in these times of troubles, crises, and doubts, opened fronts of intellectual and ideological opposition and often highly emotional ill feelings. At the end of this book, as the reader will see, I identify seven different objective "opponents": in effect, all their criticisms, echoing one another, cast a haze of doubt and suspicion over my discourse. Some people read such criticisms without reading my own writings, without even trying to find out who their authors are, and end up taking what they say at face value. If there is smoke, there is fire, the saying goes. That is quite true, but one should find out what the fire is, and who lit it.

Yet, what really matters lies beyond this smokescreen, which must absolutely be cast aside to grasp the essence of my thought and of my approach. In the present book, I deal with the issue of identity crisis and of the doubts that assail each and every one of us. I state firmly that we have multiple, moving identities, and that there is no reason—religious, legal, or cultural—a woman or a man cannot be both American or European and Muslim. Millions of individuals prove this daily. Far from the media and political tensions, a constructive, in-depth movement is under way and Islam has become a Western religion. Western Islam is a reality, just like African, Arab, or Asian Islam. Of course there is only one single Islam as far as fundamental religious principles are concerned, but it includes a variety of interpretations and a plurality of cultures. Its universality indeed stems from this capacity to integrate diversity into its fundamental oneness.

It is up to Muslim individuals to be and become committed citizens, aware of their responsibilities and rights. Beyond the minority reflex or the temptation to see themselves as victims, they have the means to accept a new age of their history. For those who were born in the West or who are citizens, it is no longer a question of "settlement" or "integration" but rather of "participation" and "contribution." My point is that we have now moved, and we must move, to the age of "post-integration" discourse: we must henceforth determine the profound, accepted meaning of belonging. This is the new "We" that I have been calling for, and that is already a reality in some local experiences.

One should not be naïve, however. Important challenges remain: I have drawn up a list as far as Muslims are concerned (the relationship between religion and culture, gender issues, the training of imams, contextualized religious education, institutionalizing their presence in society, etc.). Western and European societies, their politicians and intellectuals, must look realities in the face and, sometimes after four generations, stop speaking about the "immigrant origin" of citizens who "need to be integrated." They must reconcile themselves with politics and not act as though, in the name of culture or religion, status or social class had become inoperative or outdated references: social problems should not be "Islamized" and such issues as unemployment, social marginalization, and others should be addressed politically. Curricula must also be reassessed (especially in history but also in literature, philosophy, etc.) to become more representative of a shared history and include its wealth of remembered experience. The West must start a dialogue not only with "the other" but also with itself: an earnest, profound, and constructive dialogue.

I will deal with those issues throughout this book. I have attempted to be as clear as possible while remaining simple and methodical. This is a book of ideas, an introduction to what I believe, meant for those who really want to understand but who do not always have enough time to read and study all the books. Being an introductory work, it may not suffice to convey the complexity of a thought (which may moreover have evolved and gained in density in the course of time) but it will at least, I hope, help start an open, thorough, critical debate. This is greatly needed.

1

The Early Years

I BEGAN TO GET MORE SPECIFICALLY INVOLVED with the issue of Islam and Muslims in the world, and particularly in the West, in the late 1980s and early 1990s. Before that and for many years—since the age of eighteen—I had traveled extensively in the Third World, from South America to India and through many countries on the African continent. I had been raised in a family in which the call and meaning of faith were allied to the defense of human dignity and justice. Even though my commitment was not in the name of Islam, it had always been valued by my mother and father: fighting against poverty in the South, promoting education (for women in particular), protecting street children, visiting *favelas* and supporting social projects, fighting against corruption and dictators, and demanding more humane and more equitable trade were all just causes that they recognized and approved.

I had been a teacher, then a very young dean in a Geneva high school, and I had launched solidarity awareness operations in primary and secondary schools. A practicing believer in my private life, I respected professional discretion in my public position: I never put forward my religious affiliation. This was as it should be. Both the school system and the media praised the "exemplary work" performed in mobilizing the young for solidarity in Third World countries as well as in the West, for we had also launched awareness operations targeting extreme poverty among the underprivileged in industrialized societies and the aged: I had been elected one of the Geneva personalities of the year in 1990. As a teacher, I had written three books with my students to confront them with life, the environment, and the challenges of society: a collective work about the elderly and memory (*The Split Hourglass*), another about marginalization and academic failure (*In Red, in the Margin*), and a third about diversity (*A Common Point, Difference*). The city of Geneva had funded the projects and they had met a particularly warm and important reception. The point was to place the learning process at the heart of the city and use the teaching of French literature as a means to communicate with women and men facing social problems or simply differences. Those years taught me a lot about listening, patience, nonjudgment, and empathy. Earlier on, one of my former students had died of a drug overdose. I have never really forgotten him. I was his teacher, he taught me. He died when I was sure he had stopped using drugs. I understood that nothing is ever finally achieved and that our frailties remain . . . behind the masks of strength. Strength indeed lies in accepting one's frailties and not in persuading oneself that one has "overcome" them. But "overcoming" them may simply consist in accepting them. Thierry, my student with "difficult affection,"[1] taught me those aspects of the educational relationship. It was not easy. One day, in the conflict, he also taught me empathy and critical distance. His sister had called me because he had hit his mother. Her upper lip had got stuck between her teeth. When I reached the hospital I was angry, I could not imagine such behavior: hitting one's mother! When I walked into the waiting room, his sister rushed to me and explained that violence had been their language at home and that I had to understand: both of them had seen their father beat their mother and had experienced violence in their daily lives. "Violence was our means of communication!" she whispered to me. Suddenly I "understood" the probable causes of his attitude. I understood without accepting or justifying. To understand is not to justify: empathy makes this distinction possible and, through understanding, intelligence can help us adopt a critical stance that allows us to look for solutions. I was young and my student had thrown those truths to my face. He made me grow up. I have never forgotten those teachings, *his* lessons.

That solidarity commitment, in Geneva, Brazil, India, Senegal, or Burkina Faso, led to many rich experiences. Such personalities as the Dalai Lama, Dom Helder Camara, the Abbé Pierre, Pierre Dufresne, or Sankara of course impressed me and I owe them a lot. But even more important were the nameless: the silent brave, resisting in the dark. They taught me so much, away from media and public attention. On one occasion, I had invited a Colombian social worker to our school as part of our solidarity meetings during the lunch hour. He was to speak about the problems of injustice, poverty, and crisis in his country. I sat at the back and listened. During the first half of his talk, he spoke about traditional Colombian dances, complete with music and illustrations.

I looked on and told myself that he had misunderstood what I expected of him. Suddenly he stopped and explained to the students: I wanted to tell you about Colombian music and traditional dances so that you should know that as well as having problems, we Colombians have an identity, a dignity, traditions, and a culture, and that we laugh, and smile, and live. In thirty minutes he had taught me an unexpected lesson: never reduce the other to my perception, to his problems, his poverty, or his crises. He had taught me a lesson about the pedagogy of solidarity. I had been mistaken. After that I launched a movement in Geneva schools, calling for a true "pedagogy of solidarity." One should begin with the being, the smile, the dignity, the culture that fashions the person before reducing him to a sum of needs which "I" support. Those thirty minutes of my life radically changed my outlook on others and on life. The twists and turns of that commitment taught me so much about life, wounds, hopes, and frailties: the power of knowledge, the strength of emotion, the necessity of patience, the need to listen. I have tried daily to forget nothing.

Years later, I resigned both from my post as a dean and as president of the Helping Hand Cooperative (called Coopération Coup de Main in French) that promoted the "pedagogy of solidarity" discussed above. I needed change and to return to the sources of my faith and spirituality. Around me, moreover, the issue of Islam had taken on growing importance over the last ten years: from the Iranian revolution in 1979 to the Rushdie affair or the "Islamic headscarf" controversy in France in 1989. Islam and Muslims had become popular topics.

That was when I decided to engage in what I already considered a major challenge for the future: building bridges, explaining Islam and making it better understood, both among Muslims and in the West which I knew so well, having lived there and studied French literature and Western philosophy. My master's dissertation in philosophy was *The Notion of Suffering in Nietzsche's Philosophy*; the PhD dissertation that I had then undertaken (entitled *Nietzsche as a Historian of Philosophy*) had led me to earnest, in-depth reading of the greatest Western philosophers from Socrates, Plato, and Aristotle to Schopenhauer, through Descartes, Spinoza, Kant, Hegel, and Marx in order to confront the substance of their views with Nietzsche's sometimes very free translations and interpretations. My time was then spent on reading (and a little on sport), and I used to spend between five and eight hours a day poring over texts. I also decided to resume intensive study of the Islamic sciences. I set myself a specialized reading program, then I decided to go to Egypt with my family. Each of us was to benefit from this: my wife and children would get to know the country, learn Arabic, and study Islam. As for myself, I had set myself a demanding program aiming to cover a five-year university curriculum in twenty months. The traditional training mode (private tutoring with a scholar—`âlim) allowed for an intensive individual rhythm starting everyday at five in the morning and finishing at eleven P.M. or midnight. I will never forget this training period: it was intense, difficult, but ever so luminous and enlightening. I achieved my aims, thanks be to God, and I have since kept completing my training through reading, encounters, and of course writing articles and books about Islam in general or Islamic law and jurisprudence (*fiqh*) in particular.

The same values and the same principles that had inspired my initial commitment to solidarity, human dignity, and justice in the societies of the South as well as of the North nurtured my commitment as a Muslim. I now meant to stand up for my religion, explain it, and, above all, show that we have so much in common with Judaism and Christianity but also with the values advocated by countless humanists, atheists, and agnostics. I meant to question prejudices, to question the false constructions of Europe's past (from which Islam was supposed to have been absent), and of course, help open the way confidently to living together in harmony as our common future requires.

A point should be noted: multicultural society is a fact; there is no being for or against it. This basic truth must be highlighted before engaging in the debate over "multiculturalism," "integration," or "citizenship." Whether we want it or not, our Western societies, in the United States or Europe, Canada or Australia, are culturally diverse, as South American, African, and Asian societies have long been (and even Eastern Europe, so often overlooked when speaking of Europe). This must be accepted, and means must be sought to bring greater harmony to the "multicultural citizenship" discussed by the philosopher Charles Taylor or the sociologist Tariq Modood. The challenge of diversity requires practical solutions and compels citizens, intellectuals, and religious representatives to develop a balanced critical mind, always open to evolution, analysis, empathy, and of course self-criticism. Voicing one's own needs while also listening to and hearing the other, accepting compromise without yielding on essentials, challenging deep-set beliefs and rigid or dogmatic minds on all sides and particularly within one's own cultural and religious family: that is not easy and it requires time, patience, empathy, and determination.

I had decided to engage in that process of mediation between universes of reference, cultures, and religions. I fully accepted both my Muslim faith and my Western culture and I claimed that this is possible and that common values and hopes are more essential and more numerous than differences. Conveying that message is difficult in this time of impassioned debates dominated by confusion and mutual deafness. A mediator is a bridge, and a bridge never belongs to one side only. Thus the mediator is always a little too much "on the other side," always suspect of double loyalty. I was always "a bit too Western" for some Muslims and "a bit too Muslim" for some Westerners. On both sides of the divide, then, the bridge-mediator had to prove that he fully belonged. When passion and emotion get the upper hand and colonize debates, any balanced, critical, and self-critical intervention becomes suspect and is soon perceived as ambiguous, as an interlocutor suggested on my website. The mediator becomes the object of projections that sometimes relate to a distant past and to deep disputes and traumas. Nothing is simple. You make enemies on both sides, so to speak, and on both shores you are sometimes seen as a traitor, a "turncoat," or a manipulator specializing in "doublespeak."

For years, I have been facing such criticism, doubt, suspicion, and rejection. I have always known that such would be the price, since I set out to undermine a few certainties, to confront prejudices, and to challenge some over-simple conclusions. The political price soon became obvious as bans came in succession: I was banned from Egypt after I criticized its regime, then for similar reasons from Tunisia, Saudi Arabia, Syria, Algeria, and Libya. On the other side, I was banned from entering France for six months between November 1995 and May 1996, and my U.S. visa was revoked for no valid reason in July 2004. In both universes I had to face restrictive measures, and to this day I am often denied venues in France and sometimes in Belgium. It is never easy to mediate between two cultural and religious universes for which communication has been a problem historically, whether on the philosophical or on the political and economic level. "Values" are put to the fore, while the essence of alliances and conflicts is very often—quite simply—power.

That was the origin of the figure of the "controversial intellectual" who is always accused, "on both sides of the divide," of being unclear, dubious, unreliable—if not altogether dishonest. I have kept asking my detractors to point out the ambiguities in my positions so that I could clarify them. They sometimes did, but most of the time my detractors find it difficult to state precisely the so-called ambiguities in what I say. That is most often because they simply have not read my books and articles. Sometimes it is either self-persuasion or a deliberate intention to blur my position with a haze of suspicions, rumors, or doubts fostered by repeating the same accusations of "doublespeak" or "rhetorical skill" unsupported by any serious argument. Frequent repetition (in the media and on the web) brings lasting credibility to the doubtfulness and controversial character of the intellectual. To express that "truth," journalists and intellectuals alike often introduce me as "highly controversial," whether to protect themselves or to hint at the surrounding atmosphere.

Charles Taylor, discussing my work, once used a very apt formula: he said that I did not use "doublespeak" or "ambiguous statements" but that my discourse was clear between two highly ambiguous universes of reference. Taylor's statement epitomizes what I knew from the beginning of my commitment: coherent discourse between two universes of reference, "civilizations" and cultures, shot through with doubts, crises, inconsistencies, and power plays, must expect to come under double critical fire. At least for a while, for history shows that time levels things out and normalizes what our current fears and tensions cannot conceive.

2

A Muslim, and a "Controversial Intellectual"

INDEED, AFTER INITIAL RECOGNITION from my society and the school system, everything had now changed. The values of dignity, solidarity, and justice which I had upheld as a citizen and teacher with no apparent religion (and which had elicited such praise in the past) no longer had the same substance or worth when they were upheld by a "Muslim intellectual" or "Muslim scholar." From the very moment when I started speaking as a "Muslim" or when I was seen as such, a haze of suspicion fell over my intentions and discourse. I experienced this revelation: the heavy, age-old burden of Europe's stormy relations with religion, and in particular with Islam—including denied intellectual influence, the Crusades, and colonization—still needed to be cast off. I was a Swiss, a European, but I was above all "a Muslim" in my fellow citizens' perception: besides, I was not a "real European," or if I was, I had to prove it. My interlocutors had lists of questions that were to be put to me to "test" the real nature of my "integration" and incidentally compel me to a defensive posture of constant justification.

I observed, analyzed, and assessed the nature of inherited burdens and present fears. Continuous immigration since the Second World War, the new visibility of the younger generations of Muslims, new demands in schools and hospitals, and other issues—all those phenomena (which were soon to include violence) were liable to foster fear, suspicion, and doubt. Everywhere, the Western conscience was facing deep-set doubts: what will become of us with this onslaught of immigration which, moreover, is necessary to Western societies? Who are those Muslims who represent "a new citizenship"[2] and who are mainly faced with serious economic difficulties, while political parties know so little about them? What is it they really want: to "integrate," or to "Islamize" Europe, America, the West?

My involvement in the Western public debate over the issue of Islam was very soon to focus on the "visible intellectual" a large number of projections and/or animosities that beset me from different sides. My appeals for dialogue, for coming together through shared universals, for harmonious coexistence involving mutual enrichment, seemed "too good to be true" and were bound to "hide something." In effect, my positions were also apt to impede the interests of some ideologues, organizations, movements, and governments, for whom the presence of Islam and of confident, sometimes critical and protesting Muslims was in itself a problem and a potential danger. Over the past fifteen years, attacks have stepped up and have come from several fronts which can be fairly easily identified, as will be seen at the end of this book. The media have often relayed those criticisms either to further their own dubious agendas and objectives (when they were ideologically involved themselves) or simply repeating the allegations gathered here and there on the Internet (always the same, repeated a thousand times).

First, my lineage was attacked. Being the grandson of the founder of the Muslim Brotherhood, I was dangerous by definition and I must not be listened to. Islam, people said and still repeat, allows dissimulation (*taqiyyah*) and so I practiced it in the extreme; all that sounded so fine to Western audiences was in fact nothing but the presentable side of a far more obscure hidden agenda: I wanted to Islamize modernity, Europe and Europeans, the whole West, and I certainly had links with radicals or terrorists. Such allegations, repeated several hundred times on the Internet (without any evidence, of course), now give the impression that there must be some truth in all this. Where there is smoke, there is fire, they repeat, without trying to find out what the fire is and who is feeding it.

3

Several Fronts, Two Universes, One Discourse

My discourse faces many-sided opposition, and this obviously prevents it from being fully heard in its substance, its subtleties, and its vision for the future. Some of the criticisms expressed are of course sincere and raise legitimate questions—which I will try to answer in the present work—but others are clearly biased and attempt to pass off their selective, prejudiced hearing as "doublespeak" one should be wary of. I have long been criticizing their deliberate deafness and their ideological "double hearing": I am determined to go ahead, without wasting my time over such strategic diversions, and remain faithful to my vision, my principles, and my project.

I mean to build bridges between two universes of reference, between two (highly debatable) constructions termed Western and Islamic "civilizations" (as if those were closed, monolithic entities), and between citizens within Western societies themselves. My aim is to show, in theory and in practice, that one can be both fully Muslim and Western and that beyond our different affiliations we share many common principles and values through which it is possible to "live together" within contemporary pluralistic, multicultural societies where various religions coexist.

The essence of that approach and of the accompanying theses originated much earlier than 9/11. Neither did it come as a response to Samuel Huntington's mid-1990s positions about the "clash of civilizations" (which anyway have been largely misinterpreted). As early as the late 1980s, then in my 1992 book *Muslims in the Secular State*, I stated the first fundamentals of my beliefs about the compatibility of values and the possibility for individuals and citizens of different cultures and religions to coexist positively (and not just pacifically). Unlike what I have observed among some intellectuals and leaders, including some Muslim thinkers and religious representatives, those views were by no means a response to current events nor a change of mind produced by the post-9/11 trauma. They represent a very old stance which was confirmed, developed, and clarified in the course of time. Its substance can be found in my first books and articles in 1987–1989; those views were then built on and expanded in every book I wrote up to the present synthesis. A Muslim's religious discourse, and the mediator's role itself, bring about negative reactions in both universes of reference. What makes things more difficult is that I do not merely shed light on overlapping areas and common points between the two universes of reference but that I also call intellectuals, politicians, and religious figures to a necessary duty of consistency and self-criticism. My interlocutors do not like this latter exercise so much because indeed it is not easy.

The encounter between the West and Islam (between civilizations, nations, and/or citizens) will not be achieved constructively and positively through mere wishful thinking, by optimistically recalling the existence of common values. The problem lies further upstream. All of us should show humility, respect, and consistency. *Humility*, by admitting that nobody, no civilization or nation, holds a monopoly on universals and on the good, and that our political and social systems are not perfect; *respect* toward others because we should be convinced that their richness and achievements can be beneficial to us; and last *consistency*, because the other's presence acts like a mirror in which we should confront our own contradictions and inconsistency in the concrete, day-to-day implementation of our noblest values. This is a difficult exercise but an imperative one. Instead of unfairly comparing the ideal of our theoretical values with the other's practical deficiencies, we must compare practices, shed light on contradictions and mutual hypocrisies, and together impose a double requirement: clarifying the area of our common values and striving to be ever more faithful to them intellectually, politically, socially, and culturally. This strict, staunch commitment has caused me to be perceived as a "traitor" by some Muslims and as a "fifth column infiltrated agent" by some of my Western fellow-citizens.

To Muslims, I repeat that Islam is a great and noble religion but that all Muslims and Muslim majority societies did not in the past and do not now live up to this nobleness: critical reflection is required about faithfulness to our principles, our outlook on others, on cultures, freedom, the situation of women, and so on. *Our contradictions and ambiguities are countless.* To Westerners, I similarly repeat that the undeniable achievements of freedom and democracy should not make us forget murderous "civilizing missions," colonization, the destructive economic order, racism, discrimination, acquiescent relations with the worst dictatorships, and other failings. *Our contradictions and ambiguities are countless.* I am equally demanding and rigorous with both universes.

4

Interacting Crises

THE PROBLEM OF MUSLIM PRESENCE IN THE WEST is often presented as a problem of religions, values, and cultures that should be addressed through theological arguments, legal measures, or by highlighting some indisputable principles and values. It is wrong, however, not to take into account the psychological tensions and emotional environment that surround and sometimes shape the encounter between the West, Europe, and Muslims and Islam. Critical debate over systems of thought, values, and identities is a necessity and it must be carried out scrupulously, critically, and in depth, but its omnipresence on the European scene conceals other preoccupations that must be taken into account to avoid going after the wrong target.

Western societies in general and Europeans in particular are experiencing a very deep, multidimensional identity crisis. Its first expression stems from the twofold phenomenon of globalization and—in Europe—the emergence of the European Union, beyond reference to the nation-state. Former landmarks related to national identity, the country's memory, or specific cultural references seem to be wearing away: everywhere tensions can be felt, structuring national or regional identities are being reasserted. In addition, migratory phenomena, already mentioned above, intensify the feeling of being carried away and trapped in an irreversible logic: Europe is getting older and it needs immigrants to maintain the strength and balance of its economy; the United States, Canada, and Australia are facing similar needs—with, in addition, a long tradition of immigration. Yet, those immigrants threaten cultural homogeneity, which is already endangered by the globalization of culture and communication. This is akin to squaring the circle: economic needs are in contradiction with cultural resistances and obviously those resistances will never be strong enough to prevail. This is the second dimension of the identity crisis: here, onslaughts from outside weaken traditional landmarks. But that is not all: within societies themselves, new kinds of citizens are emerging. They used to be Asians, Africans, Turks, or Arabs, and now they are French, British, Italian, Belgian, Swedish, American, Canadian, Australian or New Zealander. Their parents used to be isolated and had come to earn a living (probably intending to go home), but now their children are increasingly "integrated" into society and more and more visible in streets, schools, firms, administrations, and on campuses. They are visible through their color, their dress, and their differences, but they speak the country's language and they are indeed French, British, Italian, Belgian, Swedish, American, Canadian, Australian, or New Zealander. Their presence from within disrupts representations and gives rise to sometimes passionate identity tensions ranging from puzzlement to sectarian or even racist rejection. Another phenomenon "from within" has emerged in recent years:

not only has insecurity or violence been found to increase in some areas or suburbs because of poor social integration, but a global phenomenon threatens national securities. From New York in September 2001 to Madrid in March 2004 or London in July 2005, the Muslim presence now imports international demands through violent, extremist Islamist networks that strike out at innocent citizens. Violent extremism strikes from within, since most of the perpetrators of those attacks were either born and raised in the West or immersed in Western culture. The experience of this violence completes the picture of this deep identity crisis: globalization, immigration, new citizenships, and social as well as extremist violence have palpable effects on Western societies' social psychology.

Doubts and fears are visible. Some far right political parties take advantage of those fears and use reassuring, populist arguments stressing nationalism and the need to revive and protect identity. Their main points are rejecting immigrants, enhancing security, and stigmatizing the new enemy that Islam stands for. Populations naturally respond to such rhetoric and all parties have to take position over those sensitive issues. This phenomenon brings about strategic shifts within former political groups: tensions emerge on right and left between those who refuse to respond to the identity crisis with stigmatizing, sectarian, or racist discourse and those who find no other means to have a political future than responding to people's fears. Lectures, debates, and books are increasingly numerous: people everywhere try to define French, British, Italian, Dutch, American, Australian identity, to identify the roots and values of Europe, America, or Australia, to find out whether cultural pluralism and multiculturalism are viable, and so on. Those questions reveal fears as well as doubts.

Similar questionings can be observed among Muslims. The identity crisis is a reality that also takes on multiple dimensions. On a global level, numerous, far-reaching questions emerge: in face of globalization, of global culture perceived as Westernization, the Muslim world is undergoing a profound crisis. Muslim majority societies mostly lag behind economically, they are generally undemocratic, and when they are rich, they fail to contribute to intellectual and / or scientific progress. It is as if the Muslim world, perceiving itself as dominated, cannot live up to its claims. Moreover, the experience of economic exile adds the concrete dimension of tensions and contradictions to this vague general feeling. The fear of losing one's religion and culture at the core of Western societies has led to natural attitudes of withdrawal and self-isolation. All immigrants have gone through similar experiences in terms of culture, but for Muslims religious questionings are also often mixed with such cultural considerations. The first generations (who were usually from modest social backgrounds in Europe, though not in the United States or Canada) experienced deep tensions, and still do: the feeling of loss regarding their original language and culture, being torn between two languages, uneasiness with the Western secular environment where religious values are so little referred to (except in the United States), relations and communication with their own children who are steeped in the Western environment, and other tensions. The identity crisis runs through generations. Here again it has to do with fears and sufferings: the fear of

self-dispossession, of losing one's landmarks, of colonization of the inner self, and of daily contradictions, with all the
personal and psychological suffering this experience entails.

One must also add to this the direct consequences of the
tense climate that has developed in the West. Repeated, accelerating crises include the Rushdie affair, the "Islamic headscarf"
controversy, terrorist attacks, the Danish cartoons, the pope's
remarks: the list is getting longer and longer and each country
also has its share of political instrumentalization, sensational
news items, and juicy stories reported in the media. Many
Muslims experience a feeling of stigmatization and constant
pressure: they feel those criticisms and this obsession with "the
problem of Islam and Muslims" as aggressions, denials of their
rights, and sometimes clearly racist and Islamophobic expres-
sions. They experience this daily: being a visible Muslim in the
West today is no easy matter. In such an atmosphere, a crisis
of confidence is inevitable: some have decided to isolate themselves, believing that there is nothing to hope for in a society
that rejects them; others have decided to become invisible by
disappearing into the crowd; last, others have committed themselves to facing the problem and opening spaces for encounter
and dialogue. Caught amid the essentially negative media
image of Islam and Muslims; the populist, sectarian discourse
of some parties; the fears and reluctance of their American,
Australian, or European fellow-citizens; and, to crown it all,
the crisis of confidence and the doubts assailing Muslims themselves, the challenge is a momentous one.

Such psychological data must be taken into account when
starting this discussion: people are afraid; they experience

tensions and doubts that often produce passionate, emotional, sometimes uncontrolled and excessive reactions. The consequences of those interacting crises can be observed everywhere: under the effect of emotion, one listens less, deafness sets in; reflections become less complex and subtle, they are expressed in binary terms and subtlety is perceived as ambiguity. Essentialized stories serve to justify final judgments about the others (one person's behavior is seen to represent all of her or his society or community). High-sounding philosophical or political arguments will have no effect if one does not take into account the real and sometimes devastating consequences of psychological tensions, of mistrust, fear, emotion, deafness, binary thinking, or of focusing on essentialized stories that serve as indisputable evidence to reject or condemn. To run against the tide of those phenomena (which once again similarly affect all parties), we need an educational approach relying on a pedagogy that takes people's psychological state into account, without trying to make them feel guilty (nor to stigmatize them) and which strives to explain, qualify, and think in mutual terms. The evolution of fear and doubt must be answered with a revolution of self-confidence and mutual trust. Emotional rejection and deafness must be answered by intellectual empathy through which negative emotions are kept at bay and subjected to constructive criticism. This requires a long-term, demanding, dialectical approach that can only be developed at the grass roots. It can only be achieved through proximity, and I believe at least fifty years will be necessary for people to get accustomed. That is a long time . . . and yet it is so short on a historical scale.

5

Swift Evolutions, Silent Revolutions

CURRENT PROBLEMS MAY SOMETIMES CAUSE US to lose sight of the historical perspective and lead to unjustified pessimism. In less than two generations, amazingly rapid evolution has been observed both in Muslims' thinking and in their understanding of the Western and European environment. Yet nothing was easy: as noted above, the first generations were often naturally isolated from an environment that they did not know well (as in the United States or Canada) or had a very modest social status and education (as in Europe or Australia). Above all, they carried with them an array of confusions that it was difficult to do away with.

The first natural attitude was to consider Western countries foreign lands where they had to live as strangers. Moreover, their perception of the meaning and fundamentals of secularism stemmed from a historical misunderstanding: for North Africans, Middle East Arabs, Asians, and Turks, secularization meant an imported system imposed by colonists or implemented by such heads of state as Kamal Atatürk, Habib Bourguiba, Hafiz al-Assad, or Saddam Hussein through dictatorial policies. Secularism and religious neutrality have mainly been perceived as processes of "de-Islamization," of opposition to religion,[3] entailing repressive measures: it was historically and factually impossible to associate "secularism" or "religious neutrality" with freedom and democratization. When arriving in the West, the first generations carried with them those perceptions and that negative burden (and they often still do). This is accompanied by major confusion between cultural elements and religious references: for many of them, being and remaining Muslims meant being Muslims as they had been in Morocco, Algeria, Egypt, Lebanon, Pakistan, or Turkey. What mattered was thus to be Moroccan, Algerian, Egyptian, Lebanese, Pakistani, or Turkish Muslims in Europe, and not merely Muslims in the West, even less Western Muslims. For many, especially among Arabs, Turks, and Africans, there could be no question of taking the host country's nationality since some day they would "go home." Some Muslim scholars (*'ulamâ*) confirmed those misgivings by claiming that living in the West could only be allowed in case of necessity: it was a legal exception (*rukhsa*) and there could be no question of settling in those countries where drinking alcohol was allowed and where religious morals were not respected.

In less than two generations perceptions have changed significantly. The vast majority of Muslims today assert their presence in the West and in Europe. Similarly, their relationship to secularism and religious neutrality has been revisited after scholars, intellectuals, and leaders understood (by studying the principles of secularism) that the separation of church and state did not mean wiping out religions but rather regulating their presence in the pluralistic (and more or less neutral) public space to ensure equality. The young no longer have qualms about taking a Western nationality, referring to themselves as committed citizens and taking part in their country's social, political, and cultural life. Millions of them are peaceful, law-abiding citizens, while the media and the public seem obsessed with suspecting a problem inherent in Islam because of a few literalists or extremists (who may or may not be violent) who claim not to recognize Western laws. Critical reflection has been started regarding original (Arab, Asian, or Turkish) cultures that do not always fully respect the fundamental principles of Islam: questionable habits, patriarchal reflexes, failure to respect women's rights, traditional practices wrongly associated with religion (excision, forced marriages, etc.) have been reconsidered.

Problems remain, of course, and new migrants are (and will be) constantly bringing to the fore old issues that the Muslims who have been present for a long time have long overcome.[4] It is also true that not all countries have reached the same level of evolution: French, British, and American Muslims have a longer experience of Western societies (American Muslims have not been there so long but are better educated) and they are far more advanced in their reflection and activities. Yet it should be noted that the process is accelerating and that other Muslim communities in all Western countries are benefiting from those achievements and are now developing their understanding of Western realities at a quicker pace. The role of some leaders who are converts to Islam is also crucial to this evolution.[5] Nowadays, people speak of being Muslims in the West and increasingly define themselves as Western or

European Muslims or as Muslim Westerners or Europeans. On the ground, activities are more and more open toward society and many scholars and leaders, women and men, build local or national bridges with their fellow-citizens and political authorities. This is indeed a silent revolution, which does not directly interest the media because it is being achieved on the long-term scale of generations. Still, once again, from the standpoint of the historical time of population movements, such evolutions are revolutionary and extraordinary. They have not been fully measured yet, and it is certain today, as I already wrote in 1996 in *To Be a European Muslim*, then in 2003 in *Western Muslims and the Future of Islam*,[6] that the Western and European experience has already had a very important impact on Islam throughout the world and of course on Muslim majority societies—an impact that will be even more considerable in the years to come.

One should not fail to observe the revival of spirituality and of the quest for meaning among Muslim Westerners. Islam is perceived as such a problem today that Muslim scholars or intellectuals are often called upon to explain what Islam is *not* in light of current challenges. However, Islam is first and foremost an answer for the majority of Muslim hearts and consciences, echoing a quest for meaning at the core of rich and industrialized societies. This is hardly ever mentioned, and yet this is where the essence of religion lies: millions of Muslim women and men experience religion as spiritual initiation, reconciliation with meaning, and quest for the liberation of their inner selves in a global world dominated by appearances and excessive possession and consumption. To be a Muslim

Westerner is also to experience the spiritual tension between a faith that calls for liberation of the inner self and a daily life that seems to contradict and imprison it. This is a difficult experience whether for a Hindu, a Buddhist, a Jew, a Christian, or a Muslim; it is a difficult experience for all human beings who wish to remain free with their values and who would also like to offer their children the instruments of their freedom. It would be worthwhile, at the core of all those debates, not to disregard that essential religious, spiritual, and philosophical dimension.

6

Multiple Identities

First an American (a European, an Australian), or a Muslim?

GLOBALIZATION, MIGRATIONS, EXILE, increasingly rapid political and social change, all these phenomena cause fear, anxiety,
and tension. Former landmarks seem outdated and fail to
provide serenity: who are we at the core of such upheavals?
The issue of identity stems from those deep disturbances.
When so many people around us, in our own society, no
longer resemble us and appear so different, we naturally
feel the need to redefine ourselves. Similarly, the experience
of being uprooted, of economic and political exile, leads to
this quest for identity at the core of an environment that is
not naturally ours. The reaction is understandable but what
should be stressed here is that it is above all a re-action to a
presence or an environment felt as foreign. Thus one defines
one's identity by reaction, by differentiation, in opposition to
what one is not, or even against others. The process is a natural
one, and it is just as natural that the approach should become
binary and eventually set a more or less constructed "identity"
against another that is projected onto "the other" or "society."
Identities defined in this manner, reactive identities, are in
essence unique and exclusive, because of the very necessity

that has given rise to them: the point is to know who one is and, clearly, who one is not.

This attitude is natural and, once again, understandable in a period of rapid upheavals, but it is unhealthy and dangerous. Attempts to clarify things are actually oversimplifying and above all reductive. Clear answers are expected from oneself and one's fellow-citizens: one should be primarily "American," "Australian," "New Zealander," "Italian," "French," "British," "Dutch"—or primarily "Jewish," "Christian," or "Muslim." Any answer that attempts to qualify this exclusive self-definition tends to be perceived as ambiguous. More fundamentally, this casts doubt on the loyalty of individuals, and particularly today of Muslims who are required to say whether they are first and foremost "Muslim" or "American," "Canadian," "South African," "Singaporian," "French," "Italian," "British" . . . The question explicitly addresses their definition of their identity whereas implicitly, and more seriously, it has to do with loyalty. Since one can only have one identity, one can only have one loyalty. A clear, unqualified, unambiguous answer must be given!

Yet the question itself is meaningless. Obsessed with the idea of defining oneself in opposition to what one is not, one ends up reducing oneself to a single identity that is supposed to tell everything. Yet there are different orders within which one will have to define oneself differently. Asking whether one is primarily "Muslim" or "American," "Australian," "Italian," "French" or "Canadian" opposes two identities and affiliations that do not belong to the same realm. In the realm of religion and philosophy, that which imparts meaning to life, a human being is first and foremost an atheist, a Buddhist, a

Jew, a Christian, or a Muslim: her or his passport or nationality cannot answer the existential question. When an individual must vote for a candidate at an election, she or he is first an American, Italian, French, or British citizen involved in national affairs. Depending on the realm or the field of activity, the individual therefore puts forward one identity or another, and that is not contradictory.

At a talk I was giving one day in Greece, at George Papandreou's invitation, the economist Amartya Sen expressed his total agreement with my thought through a fine illustration. Suppose, he said, you are a poet and a vegetarian. If you are a dinner guest, this is no time or place to insist on your identity as a poet, while if you attend a poetry circle, you are certainly not going to introduce yourself as a vegetarian, for you would be seen as eccentric. In other words, you have more than one identity and you give priority to one of those identities or the other depending on the environment or situation, without this affecting your loyalty to one order of affiliation or the other. A poet who says he is a vegetarian at a meal is no less a poet! The example is indeed enlightening, and it proves that the question of what one is foremost (or exclusively) is a bad question, a question that must be questioned and that, ultimately, one should refuse to answer.

One must resist the temptation to reduce one's identity to a single dimension that takes priority over every other. This can indeed be reassuring, but it is above all impoverishing and, in times of crisis and tension, it can lead to rejection, racism, and latent or passionate conflicts of identity, culture, or "civilization." We should reach a broader view of ourselves and our fellow-citizens: each one of us has multiple identities that she/he must accept, nurture, and develop. I have long been repeating to Muslims and to my fellow-citizens that I am Swiss by nationality, Egyptian by memory, Muslim by religion, European by culture, universalistic by principle, Moroccan and Mauritian by adoption. This is no problem whatsoever: I live with those identities, and one or the other may take the lead depending on the context or occasion. Other dimensions should even be added to those identities: being a man, having a specific social status, a job, and so on. Our identities are multiple and constantly on the move.[7]

Reaching such awareness of the fluctuating multiplicity of personal identities supposes acquiring a measure of self-confidence and trust in others. Once again, this has more to do with psychology than with philosophy and religion proper. Such work on oneself, on one's multiple affiliations and on being able to step out of one's own perspective, requires knowledge of oneself and of others confronted with daily practice: the challenge is considerable. Only educational work—genuine applied, critical pedagogy—that reconciles individuals with the different dimensions of their being, their origins, and their hopes can enable them to overcome anxious, reactive, and passionate reactions when encountering others. Natural initiation precisely needs such day-to-day, real-life encounters, around cultural or social projects, to break barriers and open prospects. Only in such daily practice, in such education through experimentation, experience, and dialogue, can one trust and be trusted and thus assess the other's loyalty. This does not mean expressing blind loyalty or having to prove one's loyalty. Trust makes it possible to understand that true loyalty is always critical: with our government, with our fellow believers or with the "ummah" (Muslim faith and spiritual community), we should never extend blind support to "our own kind" against all "others." We should be faithful to principles of justice, dignity, equality, and be able to criticize and demonstrate against our government (or even the mainstream in our society) when they undertake an unjust war, endorse apartheid, or associate with the worst dictators on earth. Similarly, we must also develop critical loyalty toward our Muslim (or other) fellow believers and oppose their ideas and actions when they betray those very principles, stigmatize the other, produce racism, or justify dictatorships, terrorist attacks, or the murder of innocents. This does not have to do with identity issues but with the coherence of conscience that unites those identities around a body of principles that must, to be fair, be used unselectively and critically as well as self-critically.

Being a patriot, feeling that one belongs to a society, a nation, or a community of faith is a good thing, but it cannot justify blind, chauvinistic nationalism, advocating a national and/or religious exception or election, or exclusivist religious dogmatism defending one's fellow believers whatever the circumstances. The most respectable attitudes were shown by those who dared take a stand against their own in the name of dignity and justice: those who, during the Second World War, refused to give up Jews (or send them back to the frontier) when their government required them to; those who refused to fight in Vietnam and were jailed for it; those who resisted unfair apartheid laws at the cost of their lives; those who opposed the instrumentalization of religion to produce very Islamic autocratic systems (as in Saudi Arabia) or who opposed the instrumentalization of its so-called modernization to justify dictatorships "in tune with modernity" (as in Tunisia); those who condemned terrorist attacks against innocents when they were perpetrated in the name of their religion.

7

Western Islam
Religion and Culture

NUMEROUS MUSLIMS—`*ulamâ* as well as ordinary believers— have opposed the idea that there could be a "Western Islam" or a "European Islam" different from the one and only "Islam." They have interpreted such terms as attempts at division, adulteration, or perhaps dangerous reform. In other circles, sociologists have claimed that there is not "one Islam" but several very different "Islams" depending on interpretations or societies and that this diversity must be addressed on a circumstantial basis. Confronted by those two contradictory approaches, my position has been to present things from within and in this manner to grasp both the unity and diversity of the Islamic universe. As regards belief, the pillars of faith (`*aqîdah*) and practice (`*ibadât*), Islam is one and unites all traditions (both Sunni and Shi'a) on the basis of the Quranic revelation and of Prophetic traditions (Sunnah) that set the common framework and principles. East and West, North and South, Muslims relate to those scriptural sources, fundamentals, and practices, and everywhere this is, palpably and visibly, what nurtures the "faith community" called the *ummah*.[8]

That being said, diversity cannot be denied, and it mainly operates on two levels. First, there is a diversity of readings and interpretations, which accounts for the different traditions, trends, and legal schools (as many as thirty at some periods). This diversity has always existed and, depending on the differences, it has always been more or less accepted (sometimes with difficulty, particularly between Sunni and Shi'a) by scholars and ordinary Muslims. The other level of diversity is cultural: the principles of Islam regarding social affairs (*mu'âmalât*) have always been very inclusive toward cultures and traditions (recognizing *al-'urf*, sound custom established before Islam): Muslims in Africa or in Asia have largely kept their way of life and habits while respecting the creed, practices, and principles shared by all Muslims. They have simply been selective and preserved what did not contradict any principle of their faith: it has been so for centuries, and this explains the notable differences in mind-sets and ways of life among Arab, African, Turkish, or Asian Muslims. Thus there is one religion, one Islam, with various interpretations and several cultures.

What happened elsewhere in the past is happening in the West today. What we call Western Islam is of exactly the same nature: it is an Islam that respects the common creed, practices, and principles and makes the various Western and European cultures its own. We are witnessing the birth of a Western Islamic culture within which Muslims remain faithful to fundamental religious principles while owning up to their Western cultures. They are both fully Muslim as to religion and fully Western as to culture, and that is no problem at all.

The point is not to create a new Islam but to reconnect Islam with its original dynamism, creativity, and confidence, which enabled the faithful to observe and integrate positively all that was good and positive in the cultures they encountered while remaining critical and selective when those cultures could result in insularity, in questionable behavior and usage, or in systematic discrimination. All cultures, whether Arab, Asian, or Western, require a critical and self-critical mind apt to assess habits in light of principles because habits often erode or blur principles. One should therefore be both open and critical: always remain curious and seek what is beautiful and good, and always remain cautiously alert in assessing what is negative and unfair.

To reach this objective, Muslims in the West and in Europe must perform a twofold work of deconstruction and reconstruction. One must first set out to distinguish what is religious and what is cultural in the way they conceive Islam when they come from Pakistan, Turkey, or Arab countries. There is no faith or religion without culture, nor any culture without a religious substrate, but religion is not culture: operating the distinction is not easy but exile makes it necessary and difficult, yet over the course of time, paradoxically, it becomes easier and easier. Initially, of course, migrants always huddle around their religion, culture, and community to protect themselves from the foreign environment. They stick to the ways of life of their countries of origin, often confusing religion, culture, and traditions. The second and later generations cannot be content with this attitude and they always (being also more educated) come to question some cultural traits of the countries of origin as they naturally absorb the language and culture of the country in which they live. This transition period is one of natural conflict between generations but also with the surrounding society: what is involved here is doing away with the habits inherent in the parents' culture that are seen as problematic and as not always Islamic, and taking as one's own the positive elements of Western cultures while remaining faithful to Islam's principles. In countries where the Muslim presence is longer established, this transition is already well under way and the stage of cultural integration has already been overcome: the young are now culturally French, British, American, South African, Singaporian, or Canadian. In other countries, the process is accelerating, and there are now increasing numbers of Muslim Westerners without this being a problem for the women and men who define themselves as such.

Western Islam is now a reality: women and men have English, French, German, or Italian as their first language; they are immersed in the various Western cultures, and despite the negative image conveyed by certain media, political trends, or lobbies, they feel at home in America, Australia, or Europe and this is where they wish to build their future and raise their children. The growing numbers of converts, who used to become "Arabized" or "Pakistanized" to feel more Muslim, have now developed into a more positive vector for the acculturation of Muslims since those converts take on responsibilities and increasingly own up to their Western and European heritage. The process is under way: Islam *is* a Western religion, in light of history, of objective data, of numbers, and also now of culture. This phenomenon, which is now patent in America,

Britain, or France, will not fail to spread throughout Europe, including countries where Muslims have arrived more recently. Even though there will always be new Muslim immigrants, the issue of Islam must now be distinguished from the phenomenon of immigration. It is henceforth a European issue, and a Western one.

8
"Cultural" Muslims, Reformists, Literalists, and So On

MOST MUSLIM WESTERNERS do not practice their religion regularly and experience no specific "religious" problems in their daily lives. Many refer to themselves as believers, abstain from alcohol and pork, observe Ramadan out of faith or family (and/or cultural) tradition, but they have no regular practice and rarely attend mosques. Others also refer to themselves as believers but do not respect the obligations and prohibitions of their religion; they may drink alcohol and live without any particular religious sensitivity (except, here again, during Ramadan, or in punctual reaction to what they may feel to be attacks or aggressions in the media or from certain political parties). Others still, a small minority, define themselves as atheistic, agnostic, or merely "cultural" Muslims (or even as "ex-Muslims") and have no actual religious affiliation. It must be stressed that those three categories (the first two in particular) represent the majority (75 percent to 80 percent depending on origins and places) of those who are defined and reckoned as "Muslims" in Western societies. Those women and men have no "religious" problem with the West: apart from their skin color, their origin, and their name, they have no "religious visibility" (nor any demands) except what the surrounding society imposes on them against their will by assimilation or projection. When they get involved in society or politics, they are still perceived as "Muslims" whether they wish to be or not, even if they do not overtly act as Muslims and have no wish to be defined as such.

Among the remaining 20 percent to 25 percent (including all those who practice more or less regularly, attend mosques, pray daily or once a week, fast, and may sometimes be involved in Islamic organizations), the reformist trend clearly holds sway from the second generation on. Some may still express traditionalist views, yet in practice most `ulamâ, leaders, and ordinary Muslims explicitly or tacitly admit that the new Western context must be taken into account and that adequate solutions must be found to face new challenges. Those believers and worshipers need to find the means to be faithful to Islamic principles while confronting the new, fluctuating realities of Western societies. This requires returning to the scriptural sources, revisiting literalist readings that proceed by reduction or "culture-based" readings that operate by projection, and engaging in new interpretations in light of the new context. Indeed fundamental principles (`aqîdah) and ritual practices (`ibadât) do not change, but one must engage in critical readings and reasoning (ijtihâd) to find the ways to a faithfulness that is not blind to the evolutions of time and to the diversity of societies. For reformists, faithfulness as to practice, prescriptions, and prohibitions is essential, but there is no faithfulness without evolution.[9]

For close to twenty-five years, I have been part of this trend that prevails among those Muslims who claim a religious affiliation and sensitivity associated to regular practice. Over one generation, an astounding evolution has taken place in text interpretations, in the understanding of the Western context, in discourses, and in views about religious, cultural, and societal debates. 'Ulamâ and their councils, intellectuals, organization leaders as well as ordinary Muslims have performed a genuine intellectual revolution: this is not always recognized in the West, for the long time of mentality change is invisible to the immediate time of media coverage (or the short time of political stakes), and yet real, highly positive progress has been made. What has been achieved is very important, as we shall see, and it brings high hopes even though the process must still be carried on beyond a reformist thought that merely strives to adapt to current circumstances (but remains unable to become a force for transformation contributing to the intellectual, scientific, and ethical reflection of which our world is in such great need). This is indeed why I call for an even deeper "radical reform" that requires us to reconsider the very sources of the fundamentals of Islamic law and jurisprudence (*usûl al-fiqh*) rather than keeping to context-related adaptations of law and jurisprudence (*fiqh*). We should thereby equip ourselves with the means to move from an "adaptation reform" to a "transformational reform" based on contribution.[10]

There are, however, literalist trends, called "*salafî*" (and inappropriately, "Wahhabite"), which have a totally different approach to the Western context. They consider that one should return to the letter of scriptural sources (the Quran and the Sunnah) and keep away from Western society that appears "devoid of religion" and "devoid of morals." The scholars and leaders in those minority trends are far from being superficial, uneducated minds: to think so would be a profound misjudgment. It is their turn of mind, a certain vision of realities, that determines their particular way of interpreting the Texts and the world: what emerges—however sophisticated their minds—is always a binary world of good and evil, of "us" versus "them," of "knowledge" and "ignorance," of Islam and others. This results in a relationship to reality as dogmatic as it is formalistic, which determines a certain way of being a Muslim today: a rigid, literalist reading of the Texts, insistence on "Islamic" knowledge that edifies as opposed to other "useless" areas of knowledge, isolation from the world which is going astray and particularly from the West, and, very often, a "literal," blind respect for ruling Islamic authorities. Those trends exist in the West and they are marginal, even though they are able to attract (temporarily, most of the time) young people looking for sharp clarity or going through crises and to whom their approach gives a sense of security. The negative media images, feelings of rejection, or social marginalization have also sometimes pushed those young people toward those trends that at the same time offer protection and enable them to construct a far more confident image of themselves and where they belong.

For those literalist trends, as indeed for traditionalists (who strictly adhere to one school of law or one ritualistic movement like the *tablighî*), reformists go too far and have sometimes "gone out of Islam." Internal debates and rejections are continuous, and often passionate and violent. In the West as well as in Asia, Africa, or Mauritius, in some Muslim majority countries or on the web, I have for instance repeatedly been called a *"kâfir"* (negator, infidel), a *"murtad"* (apostate), or an impostor seeking to adulterate Islam and destroy it from within. This happens to a large number of reformists (ironically considered "fundamentalists" by some Western circles). Other more sectarian and/or politicized trends exist, but they are quite marginal even though some of their public declarations attract media attention. The optical illusion of the media must not mislead us: the Islamic groups or groupuscules that most often make news, those that express the most incendiary and violent views, represent the tiniest fringe of the Muslim community, which does not identify with them.

One should also note the significant, inconspicuous, and often multiform presence of Sufi circles. Some are Sufi while being involved in Islamic associations, others strictly follow Islamic prescriptions and the requirements of mystics but without displaying it, others still have a very loose relationship to Islam and even to the Sufi tradition itself, with practices and rules that are very flexible if not altogether absent. This dimension of Islam is important and Sufi circles can play active, and highly contradictory, parts in Western societies (as was the case during colonization or even today in Muslim majority societies): they can stand, internally, as rigorous guardians of the spiritual substance of Islam's message; they can merely assert their autonomy from the authorities; or on the contrary, they can be instrumentalized by governments to present a certain image of the "other," "moderate" Islam, that is "free" or even "secularized"—which is, in itself, utterly meaningless.

9

Advances

For believing, observant Muslims who may have faced difficulties trying to reconcile the commands and prohibitions of their religion with life in Western societies, the evolution of thinking and mind-sets has been rapid and impressive, as I said, if one takes the time to seriously assess what has been achieved. Both on the theoretical and practical levels, a number of principles have been established and constitute advances for today and for the future.

First, the old traditional binary categorization of the world into "the abode of Islam" (*dâr al-islâm*) and "the abode of war" (*dâr al-harb*) had to be questioned. With the exception of a few literalist, traditionalist, or politicized groups, no scholarly authority and no significant organization uses those concepts anymore. Such terms as "abode of contract" (*dâr al-ʿahd* or *dâr al-ʿaqd*), "abode of treaty" (*dâr al-sulh*), or "abode of predication" (*dâr ad-daʿwah*) are now being used. I have suggested the concept of "abode of testimony" (*dâr ash-shahâdah*), which expresses the idea that Muslims, like all people of faith and convictions, should strive to be "witnesses" of their message and principles through their presence and by behaving consistently with those principles. Such an appellation breaks the binary relation and, in a global world, it achieves reconciliation with Islam's universal dimension: the whole world has become a space, an abode, of testimony. The witness is no longer a stranger in the other's world, neither is he linked to the other by a contract: he is at home, among his own kind, and he simply tries to be consistent with his beliefs and in harmony with the people with whom he lives and builds his future.

It is now clear that so long as the two basic rights (freedom of conscience and freedom of worship) are recognized and protected, as they are in all Western societies, Muslims have to respect the law, which is binding on them as it is on all other citizens and residents. Muslim Westerners have understood that when secularism and religious neutrality are not instrumentalized by ideologues or intellectual or political trends opposed to any presence of religion, they guarantee religious pluralism in Western societies and protect their legitimate rights. Once again, no recognized Muslim scholar, no credible Islamic organization, requires specific laws or exceptional treatment: closer study will show that they demand that the law be enforced and that, in its name, the different religions receive fair and equal treatment. The media or the political stage have often presented the demands of some Muslim organizations as problematic because they asked for specific rights: in effect, they were only asking for what had already been granted to others (Jews, Roman Catholics, or Protestants) before them, but such projections are made on Muslims' intentions and controversy starts so quickly that Muslim citizens' merely asking for equal treatment is quickly interpreted by the media and public opinion as a demand for special treatment.[11]

Considerable effort has gone into encouraging Muslim citizens to study and to interact more and more with society. In effect, their new visibility represents exactly the opposite of what is generally said. First-generation migrants were isolated and invisible: their presence was not even noticed. With the second and third generations emerging, things have changed: the young are now visible everywhere, in the street, on campuses, in workplaces. The first natural reaction to this new visibility is to identify it as the presence of a new, seemingly different, segregated "community." Yet it is exactly the opposite: perception by the public, politicians, and the media lags behind reality, so that they give deficient interpretations. The new visibility does not prove the existence of a closed, segregated community but exactly the opposite: it shows that new generations are opening up, reaching out of their social, cultural, and religious ghettos to take up their place in a space and society they rightly consider their own. The same is true, indeed, of African Americans in the United States. This reality is a considerable advance: at the intellectual level, in universities, on the job market, socially, politically, culturally, even in sports, Muslim citizens are getting involved. They are doing so individually, following their own aspirations and hopes, and nowhere can one find what could be considered, socially or politically, a common position, even less a representation of "the community" and of "its interests." All that is said to that effect has to do with fantasy and with the instrumentalization of fear: in reality, Muslim Americans, Europeans, or

Australians are getting involved everywhere, individually, and they lay no claim to "representing" or "defending" "the Muslim community."

One can also observe a process of institutionalization of the Muslim presence that is occurring in several directions. It naturally began with the creation of mosques: this was and everywhere remains the first act of Muslims settling in a new environment. Then associations and organizations with more or less specialized aims were created everywhere: associations for young people, for students, for women, for cultural activities or sports. Initially, Muslims naturally thought of associations exclusively addressing the religious community. They had to answer the needs of Muslims living in a new context. In certain societies where the phenomenon was well established and recognized as in Britain, the Netherlands, Scandinavia, the United States, Canada, South Africa, or Singapore, Muslims began to set up private schools. Here again, two needs were addressed: protecting the young from the Western environment (most of the time such schools targeted girls) and creating efficient schools that were not second-class schools, as state schools often are in the areas or suburbs where socially marginalized and/or Muslim populations are mainly concentrated.[12] In many countries, reflection has developed in order to set up pre-academic or academic training colleges to provide leaders or imams with solid knowledge of "theology" and Islamic law as well as understanding of the local context. One may also mention the creation of small businesses publishing books about Islam (whether new or translated), selling halal meat, or otherwise answering the community's expectations in terms of consumption. On several levels, then, a very important process of institutionalization can be observed and is gaining momentum. What is also most encouraging and positive is the parallel process of reaching out toward organizations outside the community: charities, social structures, political parties. Muslim citizens are now getting involved beyond their "community" and interacting with society in a wholly new manner: they are citizens and they are developing a sense of belonging in their daily lives. This is palpable everywhere, and it is important to take its full measure. The impact of this multidimensional process will be crucial in and for the years to come.

In recent years I have met a number of ministers, secretaries of state, and officials in many Western countries and I have put forward those analyses to them along with a few opinions about addressing the issues related to the Muslim presence. I have kept repeating that an evolution is under way and that time must be reckoned with. Nevertheless, strategies can be devised by governments to accelerate and facilitate those settlement processes, all the more so as Muslim communities are generally not rich (considering their members' social origin—apart from some American or Canadian immigrants): in all circumstances, and while respecting the legal framework of the separation of orders (state and religion), government action should be content with trying to *facilitate* evolutions trustingly and not attempt to *control* them while fostering mistrust. Any control-oriented approach will not only foster suspicion and confirm that Muslim citizens are not treated like the others: it will also fail to elicit credibility and significant support within Muslim communities.

10
Challenges

THE CHALLENGES AT HAND are numerous and, here again, multidimensional. Even though I say with force and conviction that the reformist trend holds sway in the West among Muslim communities and that understanding of the context is undergoing rapid evolution, naivety and blind optimism must be avoided. The first major challenge remains to deepen knowledge both of Islam and of Western societies among *`ulamâ*, intellectuals, association leaders, imams, and more generally ordinary Muslims. This begins with mastering the terminology: it is imperative to develop and circulate more adequate understanding of such concepts as *"fiqh," "ijtihâd"* (critical independent thinking), *"fatwa"* (legal opinion), *"jihad"* (effort, resistance), *"sharî`ah"* (the way to faithfulness) or "secularization," "secularity," "laicity," "citizenship," "democratic principles," "democratic models," "human rights," and "universals." Such concepts are read and used but confusion is widespread, and Muslims must equip themselves with clearer discourse relying on a closer mastery and definition of terms. I have been working toward this for years in the various books I have written about such issues, but there is still a long way to go before we can open a shared critical debate over concepts and their definition.

Clarifying the terminology is crucial. For example, when I state that the *sharî`ah* is not "a system" nor "a closed body of Islamic laws"[13] but rather the "Way to faithfulness to Islam's objectives" (which consist in protecting life, dignity, justice, equality, peace, Nature, etc.),[14] this entails direct consequences on my understanding of the legal framework of Western societies. Thus, all the laws that protect human life and dignity, promote justice and equality, enforce respect of Nature, and so on, are *my sharî`ah* implemented in *my* society, even though this is not a Muslim majority society or those laws have not been devised and produced by Muslim scholars. I follow the Way since those laws enable me to be faithful to its fundamental objectives and therefore to be faithful to Islam's message and principles.

Such an understanding of Islamic terminology totally reverses perspectives. Better knowledge of what citizenship implies produces similar results. Muslims must thus get rid of two obstacles that result from inadequate understanding of their status. They are faced with both a discourse and a pressure that systematically confuse orders: although they are already citizens in some countries, they are constantly considered "minorities" because their religion or their culture are being referred to whereas secularized Western societies clearly make a distinction between the citizen's legal and public status and the believer's religious affiliation. Muslims often have psychologically integrated this perception (that is projected on them) and also refer to themselves as a "minority," confusing the factual numbers of their religious community with the meaning and legal substance of their belonging as citizens. However, in the order of citizenship, of relationship to the law, or of the treatment of individuals, the minority concept is inoperative: there is no such thing as "minority citizenship"! They must therefore overcome this "minority" mind-set and fully participate in citizenship on an equal footing with the "majority." Drawing a link with the definition and the inclusive understanding of the concept of *sharî`ah* suggested above will shed light on the nature of the intellectual revolution that can emerge from this process of clarification. This work remains to be carried out everywhere in Muslim communities: the more or less clear or confused feeling that change is necessary exists, but a large-scale popularization effort is required to give it form and substance.

Such work on perceptions will make it possible to fight against the temptation for people within Muslim communities to cast themselves as victims. When it is made clear that they are at home in the West, that the Way of faithfulness to higher principles must be followed both here and elsewhere, that they must stop considering themselves a minority but that on the contrary knowing their duties as well as their rights as citizens involved in the majority is a necessity: when all that is made clear, Muslims will be called upon to take responsibility for themselves and get rid of the victim mind-set. This is a major challenge: it is urgent to stop blaming *"society-that-does-not-like-us"* or "islamophobia" or "racism" and thereby justifying guilty passivity. That such phenomena exist cannot be denied, but Muslims must tackle them by getting involved as citizens and by fighting against injustice, racism, discrimination, populist stigmatization discourse, and hypocrisies. This also means fighting against paternalistic, often neo-colonialist discourse and infantilizing treatment: for thirty years the West has seemingly been faced with "young Muslims" who are eternally "young" and who are taking quite a long time to grow into adults mature enough to discuss issues on an equal footing.

The feeling of belonging that stems from deeper knowledge of concepts and objectives is apt to enable Muslims to broaden their interests to include social problems beyond those related to Islam. Social questions, education, schooling policies, parents' associations, unemployment, the homeless, delinquency, urban violence but also societal debates, power and "race" relationships, involvement in parties, ecology, immigration policies, and international relations must interest them like all other citizens. So far only a minority of Muslim citizens reach out in this way, and they often have to face suspicion or enduring prejudice. Yet they open the way to a process that may be slow but is irreversible. The challenge is to see that this process is understood and sought rather than just suffered and managed so chaotically that it becomes counterproductive and fosters division.

Drawing up the long list of challenges is impossible, but a number immediately stand out and should be addressed as priorities. One important issue is to look into the processes through which young people are attracted to rigid literalism or, on a more political level, to radicalization, and in rare cases to violent action and extremism. Islamic education in the West must be revisited both in its form and content in light of the context and of the aforementioned challenges. Discourse about the surrounding society and Western culture must change in tone and orientation: Muslims must imperatively be encouraged to participate in the American, Australian, and European cultures (as well as South African, Mauritian, or Singaporian) that are now their own. Creativity, contribution, and production in the arts, music, cinema, and literature are to be encouraged, as well as reading all types of books. Such confident outreach, such trust in their wealth and capacity to contribute and give, such shared presence—this is what must be encouraged on several levels and in the different social, political, cultural fields as well as in sports, of course.

A word must be said here about the question of transmission because the challenge is a major one and is inadequately addressed, as reality shows daily. New generations of Muslims quickly appear and quickly become visible in society, while the ongoing migration phenomenon brings in a new population of freshly immigrated Muslims. The nagging question is crystal clear: how can advances in terms of understanding, discourse, and civic involvement be transmitted both vertically to the younger generations and horizontally to reach the different communities, and among them the immigrants who keep arriving with a vision of Islam confused with that of their countries of origin? I have already pointed out here that some populist parties use newly arrived immigrants to cast doubt on all the Muslims settled in the different countries, and the media sometimes contribute to fostering suspicion by focusing on the problems new immigrants occasionally encounter. This is a real difficulty: Muslim citizens must think out the means and methods of education and transmission in a better-organized, more efficient manner, for if they do not, advances and achievements will constantly be undermined by the attitudes of some young people or some new immigrants acting in the name of wholly deficient perceptions, or sincerely and/or naively allowing themselves to be instrumentalized.

11

The Issue of Women

THE ISSUE OF WOMEN has always been a priority in my commitment. I have kept questioning traditional interpretations and inviting Muslims to honest lucidity and critical reflection over the situation of women in Muslim majority societies and in communities settled in the West. The point was not to respond to Western criticisms by adopting a defensive (or altogether apologetic) attitude but to answer the requirement of intellectual probity and consistency. I have repeated this many times: Islam has no problem with women, but Muslims do clearly appear to have serious problems with them, and the reasons and sometimes the (questionable) justifications for this must be sought from within.

First, there is a double phenomenon at the source of all the theological and social constructions that have been established a posteriori. The issue of women is among those most widely affected by literalist readings of the Quran and of Prophetic traditions. Neglecting the fact that the Revelation took place in a given context and that its transmission over a period of twenty-three years determines an orientation as to divine pedagogy, literalist readings freeze the text out of its context, of its internal progression, and of the ends of the global message. They proceed by "reduction" and sometimes manage to justify interpretations that clearly contradict the overall message in its historical evolution or the model of behavior set by the Prophet of Islam. Beyond unjustified practices (such as physical violence as already mentioned), reformist and literalist interpretations differ in their very conception of women, and of their identity and autonomy. Literalist interpretations integrate the patriarchal context of the time without any critical distance and associate women's presence and role to their relation to men, while the reformist approach reaches out beyond the historical context to extract fundamental objectives as to women's identity and their status as autonomous beings. Women should thus become subjects and master their own fates.

The study of the writings and commentaries of early `ulamâ, from Tabarî to Abû Hâmid al-Ghazâlî, clearly shows that they were greatly influenced by their cultural environment. One can often observe that they unwittingly proceed by "projection" on the Texts, their substance and their objectives. A contemporary *faqîh* (Muslim jurist) or commentator must therefore perform a twofold dialectical analysis: the scriptural sources must first be read in light of their context, and then later commentaries must be read in light of the sociocultural contexts of the scholars who produced them. This process of deconstruction is difficult, but it makes it possible to critique the historical and cultural coating that has been projected onto primary sources. Thus, discourse about women has been widely influenced by patriarchal cultures, so that some cultural practices that were not "Islamic" have come to be justified. Female excision, forced marriages, honor crimes, for instance, are not Islamic even though certain scholars may have attempted to provide religious justification for them. This critical work is a long way from being completed, and awareness must be raised among Muslims and their fellow-citizens about those confusions that lead to the original message being betrayed. This is why I cooperated with the Muslim organization SPIOR[15] from Rotterdam in launching a European campaign against forced marriages in May 2008: the point is to speak out and state forcefully that such practices (like excision, honor crimes, and others) are against Islam.

Moreover, the psychological dimension in the debate over women should not be downplayed. The relationship to the West is a complex one: before, during, then after colonization, the issue of women has been central to power relations and political as well as theological and cultural debates. This has fostered a kind of reflex reaction in the contemporary Muslim psyche: the less Western the discourse about women, the more it is perceived as Islamic, and conversely, the more Islamic it is, the more it should be restrictive and oppose Western permissiveness whose objective is supposed to be to undermine religion and morals. Such an attitude has often prevented Muslim scholars and intellectuals from undertaking an autonomous, rigorous critique from within, stemming from a concern for reconciling Muslims with their own message and its ends. The point is not to be naïve about relations of domination but indeed to get rid of the fear and alienation that keep thought static in order to stand apart from the others and refuse their control. Refusing "Western" domination by betraying one's own religious message is an even more dangerous form of alienation since, in the process of resisting, one's critical capacity, concern for consistency, and creative energy are lost. One ends up being defined only through the others, through their negative mirror: here, psychology wins out over liberation.

It is therefore important to carry out in-depth critical work and encourage women to become involved and acquire the religious learning necessary to develop new feminine readings. Women must be present in the religious community's decision circles, in organizations, in mosque managing bodies, and other places. Things should be shaken up so that women can recover their proper place, but women themselves must also get organized: they will achieve nothing if they retain a victim mind-set. It is obvious today that wherever women have had access to schooling, have received Islamic education, or have become involved at the community or social level, they perform better than men: they achieve better results, they are more committed, more rigorous, and more earnest. Facts and figures speak for themselves. This process must go on and offer women full access to civil society and to employment with demands that should be taken for granted: similar training, similar qualification mean getting the same salary, and job discrimination (because a woman is too young and will probably have a child, or because she is too old and does not fit with the youthful "image") must be rejected and fought against. Whether or not one calls it feminist (I do not mind), this commitment for women's legitimate rights can and must take place from within to have a chance of being successful. There is a long way to go and we must all engage in it together: by elaborating a discourse that speaks of women as beings before addressing only their functions in the family or society, a discourse that protects their autonomy and freedom of being and of action. We all have to be consistent: guaranteeing women's freedom entails accepting that they might make a choice one understands or another choice one does not understand. One should be wary of those very "liberal," and above all very dogmatic, new judges who think they have a right to judge what use others should make of their freedom.

12

The Sense of Belonging and the "Post-Integration" Approach

THE FEELING OF BELONGING to Western or European societies will not spring from incantatory, idealistic discourse. Beyond all the modalities of "integration," the feeling of belonging involves very deep and sometimes complex psychological dimensions. It feeds on various elements: the surrounding atmosphere; political, intellectual, and popular discourse; media imagery; daily representations; neighbor relations; the feeling of being recognized as an asset or at least of being "valuable" in the other's eyes. It requires joint effort to nurture this feeling deep inside individuals: nothing is easy here, and all parties must take their responsibilities. If one were still to use the concept of "integration" one could, as I did in my 1993 book *Les musulmans dans la laïcité* (*Muslims in the Secular State*), speak of "integration of intimacies" to refer to the process of "feeling comfortable" and "at home." Gradually, the different modes of "integration" (linguistic, intellectual, social, legal, cultural, and religious integration) have become or are becoming obsolete: what remains is the ultimate stage, which is psychological as well as intellectual and which nurtures, and is nurtured by, the sense of belonging.

At this ultimate stage, the success of the integration process precisely lies in no longer speaking of integration. So long as one refers to "integration," one nurtures the perception of two entities based on a feeling of "us" versus "them," of a society that "receives" and of citizens who are still a little "of immigrant origin" and who are "received." The all but obsessive discourse about the "integration" of new citizens is an objective impediment to the positive development of a feeling of belonging. In this sense, at some stage integration policies result in the exact opposite of what they set out to achieve: they highlight differences, define caricatured entities, and maintain the idea that after several generations certain citizens remain guests, who are too different, who perpetually need to "adapt." Such discourse nurtures perceptions: in France or in Britain, after three, four, or even five generations, people still speak of French or British citizens "of immigrant origin." African American Muslims are still too African or too Muslim to be treated equally. How long does one remain an immigrant, while the only difference between "ethnically French" or "ethnically British" citizens and recent immigrants lies in the fact that the "ethnically French" or "ethnically British" are simply immigrants of longer standing? In the United States, African Americans still face the realities of racism, of relationships of domination, discrimination, and alienation, which stigmatize the "other." Barack Obama's election should not deceive us about the deep-lying currents that still influence and determine American society as far as the racial issue is concerned. On the scale of history, differences are relative: the problem here has to do with perceptions and representations, which produce affiliations and outline differences and exclusions.

We must elaborate a "post-integration" approach and discourse, revisiting the way in which people represent and analyze themselves and thereby taking into account the transformations in Western societies. In this respect, the history and social and political positions of African Americans are instructive and useful since their discourse and approach have overcome those registers and firmly situate themselves inside American society. That discourse and approach from within require revising our official history syllabi and suggesting an inclusive approach. We need an official history (national, European, and Western) that integrates the plural memories of the citizens (new or not) who are part of it: it is important to mention them, to shed light on their cultural and intellectual wealth, and to value their contribution and presence. No feeling of belonging to a social structure can develop if it does not acknowledge the value and the (historical and present) contribution of its members, of all its members. The point is not to produce guilt-fostering discourse about past colonization but positive, confident discourse that is able to own up to mistakes, to assess input and assets, to tell of the painful experience of slavery, of exile, and of the contribution of the first generations, the new citizens' fathers and mothers, to the construction of Western countries.

It is important to develop positive, official policies focusing on contributions and sharing rather than on a so-called integration whose meaning has become unclear now that the vast majority of citizens speak the country's language, respect laws, and, precisely, demand the right to equal treatment. Yet, all is as though they still had to prove that they belong by having to answer lists of sensitive questions (which may vary from one Western country to another) meant to establish whether or not they are "moderate" and can be "integrated." Are you first a Muslim or American, Canadian, Australian, Italian, British, or French? Do you speak the national language at home? What do you think of the "Muslim veil"? What is your position about homosexuality? How do you educate your children? Do you go to the swimming pool? Do you want Islamic schools? How do you choose your female or male doctor? and so on. Sometimes they are even questioned about the Israeli-Palestinian conflict, the war in Iraq, or more generally the crises in the Middle East, Asia, or North Africa. Such testing questions are utterly unacceptable, yet they are everywhere present and distinguish "good" from "bad" Muslims, good citizens from "suspects": and yet no one would dare ask such questions of ordinary, "purebred" citizens, of atheists, agnostics, Jews, Catholics, or Protestants, however conservative or dogmatic they might be.

Along with the above-mentioned policy regarding school syllabi, it is important to launch local projects that bring citizens together around common values and stop classifying them as "nationals," "integrated," or "to be integrated" (or as "autochthonous" or "allochthonous" as in the Netherlands). It is important to acknowledge that they are citizens and to involve them in local social actions that recognize their presence, promote their input, and mobilize their energy. During the past three years, I have taken part in an extremely interesting and innovative pilot project with the municipality of

Rotterdam, under the initial impetus of a council member from the ecologist party (Orhan Kaya). Around the generic theme *"Citizenship, identity, and sense of belonging,"* it aims at developing bridges in various fields: education, the job market, media, relations between faith communities, and social projects. The local level is where a true sense of belonging can be fostered, through mutual respect and trust and innovative, plural initiatives. After an initial cycle of encounters in the field, I have published a first-stage report about education,[16] and the process is going on about such issues as the job market and the media.[17] Just like those projects that insist on proximity, a common sense of belonging, and civic creativity—in the name of an approach that is clearly "post-integration" in nature—we need national policies for local initiatives. Besides, one can observe at the local level that the tensions and passionate debates that focus the attention of national protagonists are not part of local reality. One should not be misled by the debates in national capitals, by the declarations of some very visible politicians or of some national media who are not aware of the very constructive dynamics under way everywhere in cities and neighborhoods.

The responsibility of Muslim citizens is also very important. As I said, they must revisit both the contents of the teaching offered in organizations and mosques and the nature of the representations that are spread regarding the surrounding society. Muslim circles should insist on the importance of knowing the language and the surrounding legal framework but also develop a positive approach to culture, the arts, contributing, creativity, and of course the sense of belonging that must be acknowledged and nurtured. What Muslims hear in mosques, lectures, or community events must enable them to feel comfortable both with their affiliation to Islam and with a confident citizenship reaching out to their fellow citizens. This is why institutionalization is so important both at the local and national levels: in the long run, imams will have to be trained in the Western, European, and national context— independently, of course—and to know the language and culture of the country and be suffused with them from within in order to offer faith communities a vision and solutions attuned to the realities in the field.

Intellectuals, leaders, organization managers, and numerous Muslim scholars are making considerable efforts to effect this transition and as I said, things are moving very quickly. Nevertheless, it will still take time for Muslims to develop a consistent global vision and determine the forms and stages of the multidimensional commitments they need. Numerous challenges and far-reaching issues are involved: aside from strictly religious questions, there are of course economic and cultural considerations that must be taken into account in the processes of representation and perception of oneself and of the environment. To this should be added the political issue: at the national level, many political parties claim that religious affiliation should be distinguished from citizenship: yet on the local level one can observe that practices are quite different and that officials and representatives not only take religious affiliation into account but also rely on that feeling to attract votes or appeal to voters. This phenomenon is visible everywhere: Muslims and their numbers are, and are increasingly going to become, important stakes in elections, and political parties, often out of touch with those new citizens, frequently manage to reach them only through "community-oriented" discourse, by promising to take their "religious" demands into account. This is in complete contradiction with the political principles that claim to keep religion apart from politics. For Muslim leaders and citizens, the challenge is a major one: they can play on power struggles and on numbers to influence local policies and, at the same time, reinforce community feelings. Or they can, on the contrary, set out to develop a citizen's ethics by demanding consistency, fair social policies, and equal treatment. This means demanding political integrity, competence, and the civic evaluation of local policies rather than leading Muslim citizens into the dead end of closed, community-oriented political logics into which election-obsessed politicians are strangely and dangerously attracting them.

13

Sociopolitical Issues, the Media

WHEN POLITICIANS LACK THE IDEAS or courage to promote social policies, they simply take advantage of popular perceptions and feelings and end up "culturalizing," "religionizing," or "Islamizing" social issues. A direct or implicit link is thus established between social problems, violence, marginalization on the one hand, and individuals' skin color ("race"), cultural origin, or religion on the other hand. At a loss for political ideas, they develop expedient, populist theories that are often explicitly or implicitly racist. At the core of this process, the danger consists in Muslim citizens themselves taking in this discourse and beginning to think that their problems are not political but religious and cultural. Because they are often unaware of time-honored strategies and manipulations (power relations, representations, etc.) in the general treatment of the race issue (concerning Native Americans, African Americans, Arabs, etc.), they are all too ready—with faulty naivety—to accept the equation according to which, because of their minority religious and cultural affiliation, they will never be able to escape social marginalization. The victim feeling then appears justified, since society and its policies offer no hope: we have come full circle.

Such thinking is dangerous and must be firmly rejected. I have been repeating that the victim feeling must be fought against, but this must not prevent us from seeing that there are indeed victims of job or housing discrimination and more general racially motivated injustice. Racism is a reality and the way some cities, districts, or suburbs are managed is unfortunately reminiscent of colonial patterns, with some citizens being made to feel that they are worth less than others, that they are second-class citizens. However, recognizing that there are victims is one thing; maintaining a victim mind-set is another. I am calling for an entirely opposite attitude: because there are actual victims, people must resist any temptation to feel victimized and take it upon themselves to demand their rights.

This begins with stating that politicians must stop "culturalizing" and "Islamizing" problems because they do not know how to solve them with new, bolder social policies. Our politicians lack courage and are obsessed with the time span of elections, which is not the far longer time of social reforms. Such problems as missing social structures, unemployment, housing, or social discriminations have nothing to do with religion: they are social issues that require social policies. One cannot but rejoice that during the 2005 riots in France's suburbs, the majority of the political class abstained from turning the situation into a cultural and religious problem: the consequences could have been dramatic. However, four years on—and in spite of presidential, legislative, and local elections—nothing has been done, nothing has changed. Prudence was shown about how the riots should be qualified but this has been followed by passivity, the political class keeping silent over those issues, giving the impression that those are not the problems of true citizens, that they are not real, priority internal concerns: all is as if urban districts and suburbs were cut off from the rest of the country. In the United States, the election of the first African American president should not delude us into over-looking the structural racism and daily injustice faced by black people. Such processes of "culturalizing" or "Islamizing" social questions or conversely shifting them to a sort of civic no-man's-land can be observed in all Western countries when elections are drawing near or in times of crisis.

If to this we add the issue of immigration, the picture gets even darker. Rather than being judged in light of human rights on the one hand and economic realities on the other hand, phenomena are turned into questions of identity, reli-gion, and culture: these things are not only threatened from within but also from outside by the constant influx of immi-grants. Tendentious or clearly racist remarks are becoming increasingly common in political speeches and among people: the realms of politics and of economic management are abandoned to give way to identity-centered, "essentialist," cultural and religious considerations that justify xenophobia and rejection. In Switzerland,[18] Denmark, Spain, Germany, France, Italy, and finally throughout Europe, as well as in the United States, Canada, or Australia, Islam and Muslims do not symbolize settled citizens but eternal immigrants who are to be integrated or stigmatized. In Europe, the political issue of Turkey's integration should have been considered solely on the basis of the conditions for accession: does Turkey answer the condition for integrating with the European Union, or does it not? If it does, it can join; if it does not, it should wait and try to meet those goals. But what can be observed is here again a shift toward religion and culture: the problem of Turkey is, we are told explicitly or implicitly, a religious and cultural issue that endangers European balances and the continent's cultural homogeneity. Members of the European Parliament have said so, and governments pretend to be unaware of it: however, French president Nicolas Sarkozy has said out loud what the majority was silently thinking. The picture is a grim one, and it involves dangerous inconsistencies.

Everywhere the same displacements of social and political issues toward the cultural and religious field can be observed: unable to devise fair, egalitarian policies on the social and political levels, politicians justify inconsistencies, contradictions, and sometimes hypocrisies through racial, cultural, and religious considerations that are supposed to explain or justify differential treatment. What Muslim Western citizens must urgently demand is recognition of their status and the equal treatment that society has to provide at all levels. Social policies should be reexamined as well as the necessary management of power relationships, since this is ultimately what it is all about. The point is to accept that economic relationships should be addressed politically: because they are obsessed with identity issues and keep focusing the debate on "values," "culture," or "civilization," Western societies avoid such issues as the rule of law, equal treatment, objective relations of domination, denigration, and economic and social marginalization, of political discrimination, racism, and xenophobia. In so doing, they assent to dangerous democratic shortcomings. In the name of a reconstructed idea of its identity and of a selective and highly ideological self-representation, a huge number of intellectuals and politicians in the United States, Canada, Europe, Australia, or New Zealand seem ready to betray some of their fundamental democratic values. The danger is real.

The role of the media in representations and in the nature of national and international debates can no longer be downplayed or underrated. One can indeed remain passive and endure the "media logic" that naturally focuses on crises and amplifies problematic or negative representations; or one can think of involving journalists and the media in the general dynamics that I have been describing. This does not mean attempting to control journalists or limit their freedom of expression and analysis, but working on fundamentals and on long-term issues, first by making journalists aware that they are citizens and that they ought to keep their civic conscience alert while performing their work. This entails their focusing on processes rather than news items, on in-depth efforts to build rather than on media "scoops" and on the sensational covering of striking, shocking events. It requires "media policies" focusing on the training of journalists (about religious and cultural issues on the one hand and social issues and marginalization processes on the other hand). Local media must get involved, and interesting short- and long-term local action must get to be better known. Because they are unavoidable mediators, journalists shape representations and are in effect key protagonists in managing social, religious, and cultural pluralism, in developing a sense of common belonging, as well as in potentially nurturing fears and phobias.

Citizens, social protagonists as well as politicians, must examine the communication issue more rigorously and systematically. Leaving aside "public relations" strategies and playing on sensation and image, journalists and mediators must be encouraged to take their time, to understand the complexity of issues, and to grasp things in light of long-term processes and historical evolution. This is a difficult challenge indeed because journalists themselves are subject to the pressure of time and of majority perceptions. At any rate, we also need bold journalists who dare contradict accepted opinions, who question certainties and ask appropriate questions. They are increasingly scarce, but they exist and their contributions are essential.

14

The Roots of Europe...
and of the West

IN RECENT YEARS, the debate has been seen to shift from political and economic issues to cultural and religious ones, but it has also been projected on history, with sometimes surrealistic debates over "Western values" and "the roots" of Europe and its "Greco-Roman" or "Judeo-Christian" identity, or simply "Greek and Christian" according to the pope in his 12 September 2006 Regensburg address. With the arrival of Islam and new, more visible immigrants and with the patent change in Western societies, the temptation seems to be to close ranks, to redefine what the West and Europe are in order to be able to delimit (in the sense of setting limits to) what Western/European identity is and what constitutes it culturally and religiously. At the core of pluralism, the greatest danger would be for the idea one has always maintained about oneself to collapse: never mind the humanist values and the social and political vision of Europe and of the West; what matters henceforth is our roots, our identity, and what defines us historically as "Western," "European," or "French," "Italian," "British," or "American" in terms of ancestral culture and established religion. What this process reveals is ultimately as simple as it is explicit: Islam is "the other," even when present among us.

This idea is anything but new and the very project of Europe, beyond its geographical construction, has been nurtured and shaped by this process of distinction from—or clear opposition to—what is not itself. The selective reconstruction of historical liabilities, of Europe's roots, and the "blank" characterizing of the contribution by Islam and Muslims to the construction of Europe are edifying in this respect. The scientific, legal, philosophical, and religious input of Muslim scholars and intellectuals has been overlooked to such an extent—both in the collective memory and in school syllabi—that one cannot but see this as an ideological choice in the process leading to self-construction. To make a good impression, the figure of Averroes (twelfth century)—the *rationalist-who-is-so-much-like-us* and who rediscovered "our" Aristotle[19]—is mentioned obsessively while several dozen scientists, thinkers, philosophers, and artists are neglected although they not only lived in Europe but deeply influenced European mind-sets as well as scientific, philosophical, and even legal and political practices. Textbooks, from primary school to university, make but marginal mention of that input, and university syllabi sometimes fail to refer to them altogether. Is this partial loss of memory incidental, or does it result from a deliberate ideological and political choice? There is no doubt as to the answer.

The reflexes that can be observed today confirm the basic nature of this very old process, which consists, while determining and selecting what defines us, in highlighting what is different from us or stands in opposition to us. What we are directly witnessing today is a very voluntary reactivation of this process of redefining identity: the presence of new Muslim citizens, the continuous flow of immigrants and demographic projections cause fear, and it is therefore becoming urgent to clearly state who one is for fear that one's identity and culture will be lost in diversity or simply disappear. The fear of religious and cultural pluralism leads to reduction and to a very exclusive outlook on one's past. Indeed, those were the considerations underlying the pope's Regensburg address: by speaking about the link between faith and reason and insisting on the privileged relationship between the Greek rationalist tradition and the Christian religion, Pope Benedict XVI sought to define European (and Western) identity as primarily Christian in its faith and Greek in its philosophical reason. Islam, supposed not to recognize this relationship to reason, was thus seen as foreign to the European identity that developed out of this heritage. It was in the name of such a perception that a few years ago, then Cardinal Ratzinger had already stated his refusal of Turkey integrating Europe: being Muslim, Turkey had never been and could never be genuinely European in culture. Once again, Islam is different; it is "the other." In this respect, Benedict XVI is a very European pope who calls upon the continent's peoples to become aware of the central, inescapable character of Christianity if they are intent on not losing their identity. This message may be a legitimate one in these times of identity crisis but it is above all potentially dangerous since it operates a twofold reduction in its historical approach and in its present definition of European identity.

Europe cannot survive, and neither can the West, if it keeps striving to define itself in exclusive terms and in opposition to the other—Islam or Muslims—of whom it is afraid. What the West, including of course Europe, most needs today may not be so much dialogue with other civilizations as actual dialogue with itself. It needs to acknowledge the facets of its own self that it has too long refused to see and that even now prevent it from enhancing the wealth of its religious and philosophical traditions. The West and Europe must come to terms with the diversity of their past in order to master the necessary pluralism of their future. The reductive approach used by the pope and by those who conjure up the bugbear of dangerous cultural pluralism is of no help in this process of reappropriation. It is up to academics and intellectuals, whether Muslim or not, to prove—through historical-critical studies—that they are mistaken both historically and scientifically.[20] This would also be a means for today's Muslims to reconcile themselves with the edifying creativity of the Western and European Muslim thinkers of the past, who not only were "integrated" but who deeply contributed to both Europe and the West at large, nurturing and enriching them with their critical reflections. It is important to show that the selective memory that tends to "forget" the decisive input of such Muslim thinkers and active rationalists as al-Kindî (ninth century), al-Farabî (tenth century), Ibn Sîna (Avicenna, eleventh century), al-Ghazâlî (twelfth century), ash-Shâtibî (thirteenth century),

Ibn Khaldûn (fourteenth century), and other scientists reconstructs a Europe that misleads itself and others about its past. In light of this necessary reclamation, Muslims can show, reasonably and without polemics, that they share the essence of the values on which Europe and the West are based and that their own religious tradition has also contributed to the emergence and promotion of those values.

15

Reform and the Seven "Cs"

MY THEORETICAL AND LEGAL STUDIES as well as my work at the grass roots over the past twenty years have led me to evolve, expand my thinking, and explore new avenues. On the theoretical level, I have come to think that Muslims ought to go further than mere reflection about Islamic law and jurisprudence (*al-fiqh*). For a hundred and fifty years we have been speaking about autonomous critical reasoning (*ijtihâd*), which ought to enable us to face contemporary challenges: yet crises and obstacles remain, although considerable evolution has taken place. I believe we must now return to the sources of the fundamentals of law and jurisprudence (*usûl al-fiqh*) and question the original categorizations and methodologies. This is what I have called "radical reform," which should lead us from struggling adaptation reform to creative transformational reform.[21] The challenge is a major one and the process that can lead to those developments will take time and will initially meet sharp criticism, if not staunch opposition and rejection. The terms of the debate have nevertheless been set: my aim, along with other Muslim scholars and intellectuals, is to open a debate over fundamentals.

I have always sought to pursue this theological-legal, intellectual, and academic commitment upstream in parallel with my commitment at the core of civil societies in the West or in the Third World, and of course within Muslim societies and communities. Over the past twenty years I have been able to visit almost all European countries, the United States, Canada, Russia, Australia, New Zealand, and most African, Asian, and Arab countries. I have always been in touch with citizens of all backgrounds and religions as well as ordinary Muslims so as to listen, analyze, and try to understand. In the case of Muslim communities the world over, in the West and everywhere else, it soon became clear to me that problems had as much to do with spirituality and psychology as with strictly religious, social, or political realities.

Over the years, I have developed an approach and discourse I initially summarized in a theory of the "four Cs."[22] The idea was to set priorities and open simple, clarifying prospects as to understanding issues and getting Muslims involved. During a visit to Africa for the International Symposium of Francophone Muslims (CIMEF), which took place in Ouagadougou (Burkina Faso) in August 2006, two speakers took up the question and suggested that I add another two "Cs" to my list. They were absolutely right. Recently, after a lecture I gave at Oxford University, a woman from the audience came up to me and suggested that I should consider another "C": that, in effect, deeply echoed a conversation I had had with Karen Armstrong and had developed in my latest philosophical book.[23] That is why the approach now includes seven "Cs" that ought to be so many pillars in elaborating priorities and strategies.

What Muslims urgently need is first of all *confidence*. The identity crisis is a deep one and it is imperative, through education, to develop better knowledge of oneself and one's history, to shape a conscience and intelligence that is confident and serene: that is both sure of itself and humble toward others. Ultimately, self-*confidence* should be allied to *confidence* in others. This process must be associated with a permanent, rigorous duty of *consistency*; one should not idealize one's values and message and become unable to draw up a thorough critique of the contradictions, malfunctioning, or even betrayals that run through Muslim societies and communities. Critical mind, critical loyalty, active rationality are not only the best allies of deep spirituality but also the conditions for development and renewal. Wherever they are, in whatever region of the world, Muslims should be witnesses (*shâhid*, plur. *shuhadâ*) to the richness and positive potential of their message. To this end, they must contribute to the common welfare, whatever people's religion, status, or origin: the poor, the sick, and the oppressed, in our eyes, should have no religion. Muslim citizens' *contribution* must be an answer to the outdated discourse obsessed with "integration." In all the realms of intelligence and action (the sciences, the arts, cultures, societies, politics, economy, ecology, ethics, etc.) Muslims must recapture the energy of *creativity* and a taste for initiative and risk. Minds and talents must be liberated and women and men must be offered space for expression, experimentation, criticism, and renewal. Yet they must not forget that many of their fellow citizens (even of their fellow believers) have fears, do not understand, and would like to know more: *communication* is essential. Choosing terminology, defining concepts, being able to shift one's perspective and show intellectual (and cultural) empathy are important not only from one's own standpoint as a speaker but also in the situation of those who listen (with their fears, their history, their references). Another requirement remains: being consistent and self-critical cannot justify failure to criticize others' inconsistencies or hypocrisies. Confronted by powers, governments, or even laws (like the apartheid laws that used to be institutionalized in South Africa), one must retain one's duty and right to *contest*. One must be able to resist the betrayal of principles, even when the betrayers are one's own family, one's fellow believers, one's government, or whoever else. One must not remain silent, whether in front of the hypocritical posturing of Western states in reaction to China's repression of Tibetans (whom I have been defending for over twenty-five years) or amid the international community's silence while Palestinians suffer colonization and repression at the hands of successive Israeli governments.[24] Developing the capacity for empathy, understanding, forgiveness, and reaching *compassion* for oneself and others (as the Buddhist tradition requires) is another imperative. What this involves is not pity or passive sentimentalism but understanding and forgiveness in action, demanding justice without ever forgetting the realm of the heart and of love.[25]

The seven "Cs" (*Confidence, Consistency, Contribution, Creativity, Communication, Contestation,* and *Compassion*) provide a clear framework and above all a sense of priorities. Education, self-knowledge, critical thinking, and creativity are areas that must be urgently addressed. Muslim women and men alike are experiencing a psychological and intellectual crisis of confidence. Only through such personal efforts can Muslims learn to communicate with their environment in more than a reactive or emotional, and too often defensive, manner. That is also the necessary condition to think out contestation and strategies to resist dictatorship, domination, and discrimination not in a random, chaotic manner but with a vision that defines priorities and stages. It is urgent that in the course of this maturation process, Muslims do not allow the most radical voices to monopolize the media and public attention. *With* and *for* their fellow citizens, they must raise the voice of, and show the way to, confidence, poise, and critical rationality—but also wisdom, love, and forgiveness: remaining themselves, refusing to become "stock Arabs" or "stock Muslims," spreading peaceful, balanced, critical, generous discourse in times of crises and tension but also speaking out firmly whenever women or men, Muslim or not, betray the universal values of dignity, freedom, and justice. Demand justice and give love.

16

The West and Its Mirror
A New "We"

WESTERN SOCIETIES HAVE CHANGED and the process is irreversible. Muslim citizens have settled in and will continue to do so. Moreover, Europe's economic survival, like that of Canada, the United States, Australia, or New Zealand, is dependent on future immigration. Whatever the nature of cultural and religious resistance today, reality and needs must be considered objectively to manage current challenges in the best possible way. Discourse and policies that instrumentalize fear and play on polarization to win elections may indeed attract confused, anxious citizens in the short run, but they are dangerous, inoperative, and misleading and dishonest in the long run. Western societies must look themselves in the face, acknowledge ongoing changes, and build a new future that is not simply imposed by economic necessity but relies on definite political will, a project for society, a true "philosophy of pluralism,"[26] and a lucid outlook on cultural diversity, interculturality, and religious plurality. This is a categorical necessity: without a purposeful policy aimed at managing cultural and religious diversity within democratic societies, the very principles of democracy will be endangered, along with the fundamental assets of political pluralism in which the West justly takes pride. The issue at hand is clearly to save Europe's soul or simply to provide it with one, as suggested by the title of the program in which I took part several years ago[27] under the patronage of Jacques Delors, who was then president of the European Commission.

In front of this mirror, the first challenge is to avoid confusion. Looking beyond perceptions and imagination, the nature of problems must be more precisely defined and one must keep more strictly to facts and figures. There are religious and cultural questions that must be considered as such. There are other challenges that, as mentioned above, are socioeconomic in nature, and they must not be confused with the religious and cultural issues even though the majority of the persons involved are recent immigrants or Muslims. The overlapping and/or combination of factors (culture, religion, and social marginalization) do not make them the same: as I said, social policies must tackle social problems and they must be distinct from policies addressing cultural and religious diversity. The former will necessarily be helpful to the latter (and vice versa) but they are not identical and these realms must not be confused. Moreover, internal questions must not be confused with immigration issues that demand thorough reflection and fair and reasonable long-term policies. Women and men flee poverty, the West needs labor: how can fear be overcome to ensure that the dignity of human beings is respected and that they are not transformed into criminals and illegal immigrants while the most objective forecasts show that they will be needed? Are we going to scrupulously respect our principles and human rights or casually accept the birth of a new, modern form of unacknowledged slavery in which often undocumented workers are driven underground and then exploited, sometimes compelled to prostitution, and work illegally for shamefully low wages?

Distinguishing (and deconstructing) problems in this way may clarify issues and stakes. It should be added that facts and figures may soothe fears. Countries with the most recent, in particular Muslim, immigration should observe what happens in France or in Britain where immigrants settled longer ago. I have said this and it must be tirelessly repeated: away from media effects (because the media naturally focus on problems and crises) and political instrumentalization, virtually all Muslim citizens are law-abiding, speak the language of the country, and are involved in their society (intellectually, socially, politically, culturally, in the arts, in sports, etc.).[28] They may indeed experience tensions or, in times of crises, express uneasiness or have emotional reactions in which the nature of their responses is conditioned by the often highly biased questions they are asked;[29] but facts speak for themselves and prove that things are evolving quickly and positively. Yet this does not mean that perceptions are following suit: a study by my colleague at Erasmus University Rotterdam, Professor Han Etzinger, covering Moroccan and Turkish population groups, has shown that regarding most of the parameters used to assess integration processes,[30] considerable advances have occurred and the settling-in process is objectively going rather well, and better and better. This positive observation comes with an exactly opposite observation as far as common perceptions are concerned: people feel that the young are not integrating, that the gap between communities is widening, that Islam is indeed a problem. "Integration" is under way with the troubling paradox that in proportion and at the same time, a feeling of "insecurity" and distrust is spreading within plural society. This has been confirmed by the recent Gallup report (Gallup Coexist Index, 2009).

The distorting mirror of the media (which focus on the most extreme discourse and on the most critical situations) as well as instrumentalization by populist political parties and repeated crises all converge to keep up fear and polarization. Provocations on the one hand and excessive reactions on the other bring no relief: terrorist attacks and violence on one side, the Danish cartoons, the pope's speech, excessive remarks by some ex-Muslims or "anti-Islamic" films, from Ayan Hirsi Ali to Geert Wilders, will go on nurturing fear, mutual rejection, and prejudice for some time yet. The road will be long, and I believe it will take no less than two generations to overcome those tensions. To this end, to override fear and build the future, we must nevertheless begin to prepare the ground and make it possible for trust to develop: a real revolution of trust is indeed required to resist the evolution of distrust in our societies. I have highlighted a number of preventive measures (educational and social policies, fighting discrimination, political participation, etc.), but it is mainly on the local level that advances will increasingly occur and that success may be possible. We need national movements of local initiatives that, beyond the short run of elections, think and build for the long run.

It is on the local level that a deeper, more concrete sense of plural, creative, critical belonging can be developed: a new "We" as I called it five years ago, which materialized in a *Manifesto for a New "We"* written in 2006.[31] Our societies are awaiting the emergence of a new "We." This "We" must bring together women and men, citizens of all religions or without religion, who will jointly undertake to resolve the contradictions in their society and fight for the right to work, to housing, to respect, against racism and discrimination of all sorts or offenses against human dignity. Such a "We" would henceforth represent this coming together of citizens confident in their values, defending pluralism in their common society, respectful of plural identities, and who together wish to take up the challenge in the name of their shared ideals at the very heart of their societies. As loyal and critical citizens or residents, they join forces against shallow, emotional, or sectarian reactions. They stand firm for rationality, dialogue, listening, and a reasonable approach to complex, difficult social questions. I have said so, and let me repeat it: it is at the local level that the plural future of Western societies will be played out. It is a matter of greatest urgency to set up local initiatives where women and men of different religions, cultures, and sensitivities create spaces for mutual knowledge and shared commitment: spaces for trust. Those common projects must henceforth bring them together and give birth *in practice* to this new "We" anchored in citizenship. Indeed "intercultural" and "interfaith" dialogues are important and necessary but they cannot be as effective as shared commitment over all priority issues: education, social divides, insecurity, racism, discrimination, and other pressing matters. Governments and local authorities bear a major responsibility in this process, but at the end of the day it is up to citizens to create dynamics promoting knowledge, respect, and trust, and thereby provide direct and indirect resistance against the lures of sectarianism.

17

Criticisms and Oppositions

AS I SAID, THAT HAS BEEN MY STANCE FOR YEARS. Criticisms, first of (and mainly in) France, then taken up by some French-loving groups or some ideological currents, have built up a haze of controversy around me and my commitment.[32] Web links and blog entries have multiplied among the mass of "information" and criticism circulating on the Internet. It is not always easy to identify the numerous repetitions and allegations taken up here and there, which give the impression that there may be some truth in the facts reported, while most of the time they are merely "high-frequency repetitions" that people do not take the time to check or to subject to critical scrutiny. Moreover, they hasten to say that where there is smoke, there is fire, and that there must be some truth behind all those criticisms, reported remarks, and rumors.

One should perhaps take the time to look into the origins of that "fire," which creates such a smokescreen of suspicion around my work and commitment that they become blurred and sometimes downright invisible. What groups are so disturbed by this discourse that they are constantly striving to revive the "fire" of controversy to mislead ordinary citizens?

What ideology and/or interests do *they* defend before focusing on my own discourse and commitment? While the attacks are many and diverse, the campaigns that turn me into a "controversial intellectual" have a logic of their own and suit well-understood interests. It may be interesting to take a closer look at them.

Very Dogmatic Secularists

IN MY FIRST DEBATES IN FRANCE, it clearly appeared that some "secularist" trends were battling on the front line. For their ideologues and advocates, the new presence of Muslims and of their thinkers revived the old fears of a "return of religion," for France indeed has a double problem. On the one hand, it has a historical quarrel with "religion," and Catholicism in particular, because of which any debate about religion quickly becomes loaded, passionate, and excessive. On the other hand, the colonial experience in Algeria was a painful one, and past disputes with formerly colonized populations, with Muslims and with Islam, have still not been left behind. This was the atmosphere in which the debate over Islam flared up in the late 1980s over the issue of the "Islamic headscarf." Some highly sectarian ideologues of secularism turned it into a new religion with its principles and dogmas, reading into legal texts what they did not say (and sometimes rejecting or denying what they did say or allow). Though I was initially misled by such ideological, dogmatic discourse, I later studied the legal texts and met and debated with top French specialists (Jean Boussinesq, Emile Poulat, Jean Baubérot, and others) and I took part for several years in the Commission on Secularism and Islam of the Ligue française de l'enseignement[33] with such figures as Michel Morineau and Pierre Tournemire. This was when I understood that nothing in secularism opposed a free and autonomous practice of Islam: I have since been calling for a strict implementation of France's 1905 law on secularism, both in letter and spirit, equally for all citizens be they Muslim or not. This was precisely the position of the above-mentioned specialists of secularism, both in the Ligue française de l'enseignement and in the Ligue française des Droits de l'Homme (French Human Rights League). For the ideologues of a certain form of sectarian secularism (who are themselves "fundamentalists" as Jean Baubérot puts it) that is confused with the rejection of religion (and the hope that it may disappear), my position is unacceptable and dangerous: their own secularist dogmatism, and the militant atheism of some of them, are bent on showing at all costs that such a position "hides something" and that this is one more "religious" colonist in disguise.

Deafness is at its peak, and it has become impossible to hold a reasonable debate with some secularist groups who foster suspicion against Muslims and try to spread their doubts all over Europe and the West, through European and international institutions, for instance. A simple common sense formula that I keep repeating, such as "Compelling a woman to wear a headscarf is against Islam, and compelling her to remove it is against human rights," is inaudible in France whereas it is serenely accepted and understood in all other Western countries. Nevertheless, one should not downplay French influence over debates about Islam in Europe and the West: politicians and intellectuals upholding a secularistic ideology (by definition either antireligious or "anti-Islamic") try to spread their influence and find a number of supporters the world over, in the media as well as with some intellectuals or some political parties.

The Far Right

THE NEW MUSLIM PRESENCE IN THE WEST (resulting from immigration between the two world wars then essentially after World War II) has of course been the butt of criticism from the most nationalistic, chauvinistic, and sometimes clearly racist parties. As I said, the increasingly visible presence of the younger generations of Muslims throughout the West, continuous immigration, and the identity and confidence crisis of nation-states amid globalization have been ideal targets for far right populists denouncing the danger of foreign presence. In the past that danger used to be, here and there on the same continent, Italians, Spaniards, Portuguese, Poles, Blacks, and others. Then people increasingly began to speak about Arabs, Pakistanis, Turks, Bosnians, Kosovars, and Albanians, and assimilate them to "Islam" and "Muslims" who were endangering the identity and homogeneity of Greco-Roman and Judeo-Christian "Western and European culture."[34]

What is disquieting today is that what used to be said exclusively by far right politicians and intellectuals has now become standard discourse among more traditional parties right and left. Statements about immigration, assimilation, Muslims being "impossible to integrate," the incompatibility of values or "cultures," essentialism in the representation of "Muslims" are so many references and clichés that often stem from racism and sometimes recall the darkest periods of the West's history. What used to be said about Jews (doublespeak, double allegiance, and obscure connections with "international Judaism") is now reproduced in almost similar terms about Muslims: the comparison is most disquieting, and yet what is shocking is the breadth and "transversality" of this discourse, which now transcends ideological and political affiliations. Lacking innovative and efficient social policies, many parties have no qualms about playing on fears and in the populist vein, especially at election times, with closed discourse about "national identity" and "security" and very biased statements about immigrants and foreigners or, more explicitly, about Muslims and their practices.

Some Feminist Trends

MANY TRENDS OF FEMINISM were originally quite close to progressive Christian circles. Others stood out by their staunch opposition to religion, which they saw as intrinsically producing patriarchal discourse that discriminated against women. In former Communist or Socialist environments, feminism was naturally associated with a radical critique of religion (Christianity essentially) said to foster a negative image of women, reinforce inequalities, and oppose women's liberation, in particular by prohibiting contraception and abortion.

The new Muslim presence, along with the visibility of Muslim women wearing headscarves, and sometimes even the "niqab" (veil covering the face), has intensified fears of a return to religion, necessarily opposed to women, their status, and their autonomy. Although during the Middle Ages and Renaissance and until the eighteenth century Islam and Muslims were thought to have a particular taste for sensuality and "lewdness" in keeping with the stereotyped Oriental universe of the *Arabian Nights*, colonization and the post-colonial period brought the totally contrasting image of a strict, unsophisticated religion, opposed to women's bodies and to pleasures. It will be noticed that in both historical periods, Islam was always pictured as "the other," "different," "antithetical": the conservative Christian West pictured Islam as lewd and permissive; the free modern West depicts a caricature of Islam focusing on prohibitions and sexual oppression.

Feminist organizations have split up throughout the West. Some groups have established links with Muslim organizations (in Europe, Canada, Australia, the United States, and South Africa as well as Muslim majority countries): they deem it possible to find common points between their commitment and the struggle of women who want to remain Muslim and fight from within Islam to further their causes against literalist and/or cultural interpretations. Others cannot accept such alliances and carry on their feminist struggles exclusively with "ex-Muslims" or simply against Islam, which they see as intrinsically discriminating...like all religions, or perhaps a little more. The idea that a woman might find liberation in and through Islam, as I have been suggesting for years, is simply meaningless to them, and those who spread such an idea can only be manipulators. To those "Western feminists" (who often believe that they alone hold the monopoly of universal values and feminism), the struggle of Muslim women, or "Islamic feminism," is a fraud, and they try to discredit any discourse supporting its positions: the Muslim headscarf can only be a symbol of male oppression and the only true and legitimate feminism is that developed by Western women. This is clearly a Western-centered view and, with the irony of terminology, paternalism looms large.

Some Homosexual Groups

Homosexual organizations display the same apprehensions about religions in general as can be observed in some secularist and feminist circles. Religions generally condemn homosexuality, and the return of religion, and particularly of Islam, is thought to imply that discourses of condemnation, rejection, or of passive and active homophobia will reappear. Recent years have seen the birth of actual lobbies of gay and lesbian organizations that intervene in politics and in the media to denounce the reality of homophobia in Islamic circles, especially in the books and discourse present in the West (and in the East), and point out the danger lurking in the very principles of Islam. Islam's and Muslims' capacity to "become modern" will, according to them, lie in their capacity to accept homosexuality and not condemn it. Some of them expect Muslims to acknowledge homosexual marriage and adoption and to accept the possibility that an imam might be homosexual. This is the price for Muslims to be truly integrated and any other discourse will inevitably be held in suspicion.

There are of course discourses of condemnation, and others explicitly homophobic, within Muslim majority societies and among individuals living in the West. It would be wrong to deny it. However, various approaches exist and the different positions present among Muslims must be noted. I have been repeating for years that Islam does not promote homosexuality (it is rejected in principle since it does not correspond to the divine project established for all human beings), but that does not prevent me from having a clear position: not sharing the opinions and actions of homosexuals as to their sexuality does not prevent me from respecting who they are. This is indeed what each of us should expect from fellow human beings: respect as a being even though there may be disagreement over belief and / or behavior. Though I have reservations about homosexual couples marrying or adopting children, I do not hesitate to fight against the homophobic discourse or measures of which they may be the victims and to get involved in all common causes by their side. Some homosexual organizations still find this discourse too "conservative" as well as dangerous because of its apparent openness. They see only one possible future for coexistence with Muslims: promoting and allying themselves with Muslim gay and lesbian organizations. Those scholars and Muslims who respect beings without promoting their sexual behavior do not go far enough for their all-out, often quite outspoken militancy.

Pro-Israeli and Neoconservative Circles

THE ISRAELI-PALESTINIAN CONFLICT is a central issue and its impact has become global. Two phenomena linked to the situation in the Middle East have appeared in recent years and have a major effect on Muslim settlement in the West. They must be identified and fully assessed. First, there is what has been termed the rise of a "new anti-Semitism" that is said to originate no longer in far right parties but among Arab, Asian, Turkish, and Muslim residents or new citizens. Jewish organizations and intellectuals, in France, Germany, Britain, Australia, Canada, or the United States, have denounced the emergence of this phenomenon, sometimes stigmatizing Muslim populations living in the West. The presence of new Muslim citizens has also resulted in increasingly critical discourse about Israel's policies and its treatment of the Palestinian population. More and more intellectuals and organization leaders of Arab, African, or Asian descent (mainly but not exclusively Muslims) have developed a position on successive Israeli governments and have rallied left-wing, far left, or altermondialist (but also right-wing and center-right) political movements that criticize Israeli policies.

Thus, the Muslim presence has been described by some organizations or intellectuals (both Jewish and non-Jewish) as a danger threatening to revive the old demons of anti-Semitism in the West. Some have added to that threat one of an anti-Israeli "Islamo-leftism," claiming that the latter revealed its deeply anti-Semitic nature. I was among the first, as early as 1992, to speak out against anti-Semitism among Muslims: I said that "anti-Semitism was by essence anti-Islamic" and that one had to denounce the deviations that could be found in some Muslim discourses justifying the rejection of Jews on the grounds of the oppression carried out by Israeli governments. In the meantime, I decided not to remain silent and to reject all forms of black-mail: criticizing Israel and its continuous colonization, annexation, and oppression policies is not anti-Semitism; neither does criticizing the Saudi Arabian government have anything to do with Islamophobia. Things must be kept separate: one should reject anti-Semitism in all its aspects but draw up a clear and necessary critique of Israeli poli-cies. That is precisely the meaning of the principles of the Global Movement of Non-Violent Resistance[35] that we launched with intellectuals and organizations the world over (of all political and religious affiliations) as a result of the attack on Gaza in December 2008–January 2009: on the one hand, staunch rejection of all injustices; on the other hand, unfailing opposition to all racisms.

Such discourse is considered dangerous by all the uncon-ditional supporters of Israel and its policy. To prevent the critique from being heard, the simplest way is to cast a suspicion of anti-Semitism over all those who question Israeli policies. Many others, along with me, have endured the anger and manipulations of certain pro-Israeli lobbies. In 2003 I spoke out against the maneuvers of some (Jewish and non-Jewish) intellectuals who denounced the new anti-Semitism and stigmatized its new promoters as "Arabs," "Asians," and more generally "Muslims." I also said that the influence of pro-Israeli lobbies was important in promoting the war in Iraq, both in Europe and in the United States,[36] and that this was in itself a problem and a danger. I should also have mentioned the considerable influence of Evangelical Christian Zionists. Be that as it may, my taking this double stand set off a slander campaign in France and in the United States (then in Europe as a result of the French campaign): I was presented as an "anti-Semite" who denied Israel's existence or wanted it destroyed. My position also led to my U.S. visa being revoked nine days before I was to move permanently to Indiana to take up a dual professorship at Notre Dame University.[37]

Beyond those incidents, one must remember the reality of the general climate and of political games and tactics: numerous Israeli lobbies work at spreading suspicion toward the Muslim presence—seen as potentially anti-Semite—and try to associate any criticism of Israeli policies coming from Arab and Muslim (but also Christian) intellectuals with the same dangerous anti-Semitism. Some Israelis and Jews have denounced this unwholesome game, but they run against the tide and they have been labeled "self-hating" Jews.

Some Arab and ... Western States

THE PICTURE WOULD NOT BE COMPLETE if one did not add the tactics employed by certain Arab governments. They are also fearful of all the voices that, living in the West, can criticize dictatorship, lack of democracy, the absence of civil societies, torture, and the oppression of populations. Such states as Saudi Arabia, Egypt, Syria, Tunisia, Algeria (and so many others) keep interfering through direct political or diplomatic means to vilify the Muslim scholars, intellectuals, or leaders who criticize them. Those are supposed to be patently dangerous women and men, who maintain links to Islamism (whether radical or not) while pretending to be democrats. It is in those countries' interests to cast a haze of suspicion over figures who might make themselves heard in the West since, having definitely settled in democracies, they are free and they no longer need to "return to their home countries."

Surveillance by foreign embassies, information about so-called suspects, or "rumors" about the reliability and loyalty of this or that association leader or intellectual are common practice: that is the daily lot of many Western citizens involved in Muslim associations. Over time, Western governments will certainly become less dependent on foreign sources of information, but for the time being, "very democratic" Arab states keep fostering rumor and suspicion about their opponents living abroad, and Western leaders (as well as some journalists who are regular guests at press dinners) receive that useful, "firsthand" information.

It should be added that some Western governments themselves are not very happy with their Muslim citizens and residents criticizing the duplicity of their policies when they speak
of democracy and do not hesitate to collaborate with the
worst dictatorships if they are rich or geo-strategically interesting. Fostering suspicion about those Muslim intellectuals'
and leaders' commitment and intentions may also reduce the
impact of their internal political criticisms. There is an objective alliance of well-understood interests between some autocratic Arab and Asian states and some Western governments
who collaborate with them, in complete contradiction of the
values they claim to endorse and promote (human rights,
democracy, etc.).

Some Salafî *Groups and Some "Ex-Muslims"*

ONE MUST NOT FORGET THE OBSTACLES AND CRITICISMS that
come from within Muslim communities in the West and what
advantage can be taken of them. The picture becomes all the
more complex when one fully measures the internal tensions
and divisions that are far from clarifying things and that may
be used politically in one way or another.

Thus literalist *salafî* groups or highly traditionalist movements generally avoid getting involved in politics while they
often elaborate a very harsh theological discourse toward
reformist and/or Islamist movements. Some of those literalist
salafî groups support such states as Saudi Arabia, being
convinced that one must respect the authority of governments

which, according to them, "implement Islam." Though they are no doubt religiously sincere, their political naivety is as profound as it is dangerous. Those groups or their criticisms may be exploited in the West to cast suspicion or disrepute on other currents. Elsewhere, in painful circumstances, this very peculiar play of alliances could be observed with the Taliban: after being useful to American goals in Afghanistan for a while, they became everybody's enemies as soon as the Bush administration changed their minds about them.[38] Similar strategic instrumentalization exists, on another level, in Western societies where Muslim leaders or governments deliberately exploit such divisions and some people's political naivety.

One should also add to this the efforts and criticisms of those who still refer to themselves as Muslims or "cultural Muslims" or who call themselves "ex-Muslims," and whose current or past affiliation to Islam grants their speech some credibility. Some of them have gone through difficult experiences within Muslim societies or communities; others used to be radicals or violent extremists, while others come from Muslim majority societies and claim to know the true nature of problems "from within." Some of their criticisms are undoubtedly justified and relevant, and they must be answered. Yet what is obvious today is the exploitation of such "insider discourse" that is supposed to prove the danger of Islam, the duplicity of some Muslims, or the secret ramifications of a "sprawling Islamist International." Deliberately or not (and sometimes with full awareness), those "moderate Muslims" or those "ex-Muslims" (who gain recognition, fame, and some financial benefit) go along with certain governments' tactics or ally themselves with supposedly "ideologically neutral" intellectuals to foster suspicion and confirm doubts about Islam or about some Muslim scholars or intellectuals.

If some Muslims say it, it must be true! Once again, the point is not to claim that all their criticism is groundless but to be fully aware of the potential political exploitation of such discourse: some of those Muslims or "ex-Muslims"[39] have moreover understood that they only have to repeat what people want to hear, and they are happy to oblige.

As can be seen, the criticisms directed at me are varied and diverse. When one considers an intellectual presented as "controversial" and takes stock of the amount of criticism that seems to come from all sides, having some doubt and suspicion is normal. Yet one should go further and not only question the target but also analyze the ideological dispositions and the intentions of the different sources that produce those criticisms, foster rumors, and repeat allegations. Then, one stops being naïve. Once again, my point is not to deny the legitimacy of some necessary and relevant questions. But one must not maintain a political naivety that prevents debate, makes one deaf to arguments, and most of all, causes our democratic spaces and our respective capacities for fruitful and constructive exchanges of ideas to slowly disintegrate. The "fires" that produce thick, rarely innocent, often strategic smoke should therefore be carefully scrutinized. They should be known and identified; and when they involve dishonesty, lies, or manipulation, they should be ignored. As far as I am concerned, I go on with my commitment, with my efforts to make things clear and to communicate, resisting injustice, fighting against racism, political lies, and ideological over-simplicity: I know where some attacks come from and I also know that my path invites me to put them into perspective, or even to brush them aside, with determination and wisdom. I have learned that one should say "Peace!" to those who shout their hatred for one's being and presence or at one's passage. That is not always easy. Such is the meaning of all spiritualities, the deep *jihad* of the heart and mind. So I say "Peace," with force, tranquility, and dignity, to all the instigators of lies, hypocrisies, and wars.

Conclusion

THE READER MAY BY NOW HAVE REALIZED that my fields of activity are multiple, complex, and often complementary. My addressing a variety of issues in different fields or realms may have led to confusion, along with opposition and criticism. I am aware of this and I have often had to make it clear from what standpoint and with what status I was speaking. Was it as man of religion? Among religious trends, was I a reformist or a conservative? Did I speak as a Westerner, or as a citizen of which country? Politically, was I rather to the left or to the center of the political spectrum?—and so on and so forth. Some commentators have found it difficult to situate me, and this is understandable because of the variety of topics addressed (religious, cultural, social, philosophical, and political, national, and international) and of the complexity of the issues. Yet this is what being a committed intellectual involves, and it would be contradictory to expect a "Muslim intellectual" to speak about nothing but Islam; or to decide that his being a "Muslim" is enough to cast suspicion on his political commitment and discourse which of course by definition cannot be free, autonomous, and even less, universalistic. An openly Muslim Western intellectual is after all most unsettling: he reflects to Western society a mirror of not always acknowledged contradictions or, by his mere presence, reveals unconscious Western-centrism with its suppressions, its hang-ups, possibly its traumas. I have occasionally had live personal experience of the tense, obsessive reactions or obvious faulty acts that could result from my presence in certain societal debates—from which I should probably have been naturally absent. I have seen intelligent, educated women and men, endowed with perfect hearing, actually become deaf . . . and suddenly less intelligent, and sometimes not educated at all. My study of psychology and psychoanalysis, with the help of critical distance and sometimes humor, have enabled me to understand such symbolical transfers and negative sublimation.

Nevertheless, I remain fundamentally optimistic while knowing, as I said, that the road will be long and that evolutions and progress must be considered in terms of generations rather than of years. Efforts are required in many fields and we must get involved, steadfastly and consistently, in accelerating and accompanying the transformation processes. For twenty-five years I have kept trying, both on the academic and theoretical level and very practically at the grass roots, to set forth a vision, nurture reflection, and test strategies and projects. Everywhere in the West, advances must be recorded and a thorough assessment of the situation and of remaining challenges must be carried out in every country. By putting forward a few ideas, this book has also outlined prospects for present and future commitments. This also must be discussed and debated earnestly, without undue passion or excessive emotion.

As I have repeatedly stated, the challenge is also a psychological one. We must learn and recapture the meaning of self-confidence and of trust in others. This requires considerable effort from everyone: facing one's fears, studying, questioning one's position, telling and conveying what one is but also listening and reaching out of oneself to meet others. Self-confidence and trust in others require that both parties be lucid as to their own difficulties and genuinely seek knowledge and understanding. Such an effort involves resisting one's own fears, phobias, and distrust to reach a state of knowledge, mastery, and fulfillment, and to achieve self-respect and respect for others: for everyone, Muslims and non-Muslims, this is genuine *jihad*, in the very precise meaning this term has in Islamic references (effort and resistance), a *jihad* for trust. This is a daily effort, with oneself and with one's neighbors, in one's home and in one's neighborhood: this is how the pluralism of ideas, cultures, and religions should be managed if we want to give unity to diversity or simply give a meaning to our living together. This is by no means easy and it will never be, but we actually have no choice: like every conscience or society at a specific time in history, we are facing the key requirement of our time.

It is difficult, in these times of global communication and culture, of speed, sometimes of haste and collective emotionalism to take the time to reconcile ourselves with the slow, dense time of critical reason, of knowledge, understanding, and complexity. Experience has shown me, both with young and older people, that day-to-day mingling and personal involvement is what awakens minds, brings awareness, and spurs the desire to go further, to understand better, and to carry out a dialogue. This is why we must *really* live and work *together* on *shared* projects.

The question is in effect simple. Over and beyond all the theories that could be devised, it is important to ask everyone, as I often do when concluding lectures: how many women and men from outside your "own circle," your "own culture," or your "own universe of reference" have you met during the past month?[40] With how many of them have you exchanged views, debated, or even worked at a common social, cultural, or political project? How many women and men have you met in the past month, or two or six months, with whom you have experienced cultural, religious, and social diversity, been positively questioned, and been compelled to reconsider your way of thinking, your certainties, and your habits as well as some of your prejudgments and prejudices? It is easy to think of oneself as "open" in a universe peopled with always the same citizens and friends, and where openness is thought rather than actually experienced. Mental ghettos are not mirages; they actually exist in palpable reality: being "open" inside one's mental or intellectual ghetto does not open its door but simply allows one to harbor the illusion that there is no ghetto and no door. The most dangerous prisons are those with invisible bars.

Reaching out of the mental, intellectual, but also social, cultural, and religious ghetto is of course a fundamental requirement for Muslims as well. I have often repeated to Muslim Westerners that they should think of themselves as "gifts" as well as "questions" to their fellow citizens. They are gifts because they carry with them other prospects, other cultures, and other memories that are a wealth with which they nurture their own society. They must be aware of and consider confidently what they are and what they can bring to Western societies: other viewpoints, the experience of true cultural pluralism, the meaning of shared, and not monopolized, universals. This presence from within is now a constitutive element and suggests that advances in economic development and technological skill should never be mistaken to imply ideological or philosophical superiority. This presence and gift offers its wealth and teaches humility. But Muslims must also remain "questions": with their faith, their practices, their behavior, and their day-to-day civic commitment, they must positively challenge their fellow citizens. This is exactly the meaning of the formula I used many years ago when I told Muslims: your presence must become normal without becoming commonplace. Learning to cope with the spiritual quest for the divine, for oneself, and for meaning at the core of Western societies, when one has chosen to, is not commonplace. Thinking and living out this quest by practicing a daily ethics that shapes one's conscience and heart and orients one's actions is not trivial. Developing an *ethics of citizenship* that requires consistency and relies on reconciliation between the universality of values and the sense of belonging (and critical loyalty) on the national and local level is not commonplace. At the core of the West, Muslims' individual and collective presence should be seen as a question or rather a series of questions: What does this presence mean to me? How can their behavior be explained? Where do I stand? Who am I and what do I want to be in front of this "other," at the core of shared, confident pluralism? This questioning presence is a mirror. The mirror of the other reflects a thousand questions about oneself. Those questions may indeed be unsettling at times, but they are ever so necessary.

It will take time; it will take patience. Genuine, impressive advances have already been achieved. Beyond the crises in the media and politics, new dynamics emerge, initiatives and interesting projects bring together women and men who refuse polarization, simplification, manipulation, and exclusion: politicians and social workers (locally or nationally), responsible and conscientious journalists, ordinary and/or anonymous citizens. Those women and men are far more numerous than is generally believed, and they share a certain sense of humanity, dignity, and ethics, whether they are believers or not, Muslims or not. It is with those women and men that the future must be built, without naivety, but with trust and determination.

Appendix I
Thierry

AT THE BACK OF THE CLASSROOM, he had kept his coat on; as if he was about to leave. Yet we had just got in. That was the first time I met Thierry. Later encounters gave rise to a particularly tense conflict. Alone, both feverish and proud, he kept trying to show me that my position as a teacher was enough to prove that "I could not understand," that of course "I judged him"... badly, like "them." All my "teacher's" demands, all my attempts at dialogue, all my suggestions were brushed aside with the coldness and hatred shown to enemies. "Mind your own business... I don't want to talk to you..." He was scornful to excess—"asocial," they said.

Then, the day before the autumn break, as he handed in a French essay, he told me: "It must bother you to read our essays during the holidays?!" He was watching me, as if to take immediate note of my reaction to the challenge. "Of course, my dear Thierry..." I answered, looking straight at him. He was embarrassed, but this was the first exchange, the first "warmth," the first sign. "See you," he said, as he turned away with a strained smile. Affection was so difficult for him.

The following weeks and months allowed me to chart Thierry's background. Too many absences, too much violence had undermined all his protections. He was ever so fragile and withdrawn that he ended up turning his weakness into a strength: he did not allow anyone to love him. At best, he accepted to be judged, at school...and very badly. He was so used to it that he made a point of strengthening that image: he knew how to show adults how worthless he was, from teachers to the young offenders department. With the painful paradox that he was a victim of what he thought he decided.

There were drugs and theft; running away and wandering. Then, more and more often, signs showed that a bond was forming through the successive failures. Thierry tested my trust and my patience, and with unsettling regularity he failed to respond to the slightest of my human demands. He needed to be loved beyond the law, beyond norms, at the far end of transgression...Otherwise, there could be no love! His broken home, his solitude had taught him that those who give normal love can easily betray it. The nature of his fate had overshadowed school expectations: where others learned, Thierry stumbled. Where others found their way, he lost his.

THIERRY TAUGHT ME THE SADNESS of paths outlined very early on. I became aware, in the most violent manner, that some teenagers earn life through an infernal inner struggle. Between survival and school, the choice is obvious. Emptiness served as an identity in Thierry's conscience, what was there to train? His doubts and mine taught me to be there and say nothing.

He demanded silence. He had turned me into a teacher who had nothing to say. I was supposed to give "knowledge"; I had to experience the ignorance of a collapse.

The darkness tore apart when we traveled to Mali together. There were three of us and Thierry was among us. He stopped "smoking"...for a month, he marveled. "Here, it is worth it somehow..." Strangely, he felt that he was becoming part of a background that responded with sympathy, no questions asked. His will was suddenly brimming with resources: "I'm starting again from scratch....I'm going to get what I was not given." Today those words echo in my memory. When we got back, and for six months, Thierry lived on that hope, on that strength. We had "won"...

And then, all was empty. Thierry was lying at the foot of a tree when he was found dead, in the autumn of 1983. The trap of his life had snapped shut: an overdose, quite simply. Images, horizons crowd into my mind. And a testimonial, a tribute, a gesture. Thierry shaped my fate as a teacher. He had not chosen anything, and all doors had closed. Even before he was born, he had been condemned, to be born condemned. Like all those around him, I was necessary to him, and insufficient. His death at nineteen colored my commitment with a require-ment: to be there above all, come what may. Without a heart our profession is no longer one. What remains is to overcome failures. Thierry is no more. A memory; images from which, with a few doubts, one should draw the strength to go on.

Appendix II
Manifesto for a New "We"
*An Appeal to Western Muslims and
Their Fellow Citizens*

WE HAVE AMPLE REASON TO BE CONCERNED. The situation of Muslims in Western societies has, for the last twenty years, been fraught with difficulty. If anything, this situation has worsened over the last five years. The "war against terror" launched after the events of September 11, 2001, along with repeated terrorist attacks throughout the world and increased tensions arising from social problems or from immigration, have combined to portray Islam—and Muslims in general—as a threat to Western societies. Fear, with the emotional and often irrational reactions that accompany it, has become a part of the public mind-set. While such reactions may sometimes be legitimate and understandable, they are also being exploited with increasing frequency for political and electoral ends.

From Canada to Australia, by way of the United States and Europe, hardly a Western society has been spared its own searing questions of "identity," its own "integration"-related tensions, and its own debate on the place of Muslims within its confines. Muslims, meanwhile, realize that the atmosphere has become more highly charged, that suspicions have deepened; they have become the subject of debates that are neither entirely transparent nor very healthy. Muslims find them-selves faced with clear-cut alternatives: they can accept their lot and adopt the attitude of the "victim," the "discriminated minority," who withdraws into itself and never ceases to justify itself, or they can face up to their difficulties, become full-fledged subjects of their own history, and take the necessary corrective measures. It is only natural that they complain of the treatment handed them, that they criticize the racism and daily discrimination they must endure, but in the final analysis, their fate is in their hands. Nothing will change until they accept full responsibility for themselves, become constructively critical, and self-critical, and respond to the creeping evolution of fear with a firmly grounded revolution of trust.

Handling Fears; Facing Legitimate Questions

EVENTS OF RECENT YEARS have brought Western populations face to face with new realities and self-doubts as deep as they have been challenging. The increasingly visible presence of millions of Muslims in their midst has made them aware that their societies have changed: cultural homogeneity is a thing of the past, the question of their own identity has become complex, social mixing is an ideal that can only be achieved with difficulty, particularly when social problems such as unemployment, racism, and marginalization multiply. This sense of instability, combined with the presence of a reli-gion and a culture seen as "foreign," has given rise to fears and to questions that are perfectly legitimate, even though they may be expressed with a certain confusion. Are Muslims truly capable of living in secularized societies? Are their values compatible with those of democracy? Can they live side by side and mingle with their non-Muslim neighbors? Can they combat the shocking behavior exhibited in their name, in the form of terrorism, domestic violence, forced marriage, and the like? Can they free themselves from their social ghettos, those breeding grounds of unemployment, insecurity, and marginality?

Faced with these questions, Muslims must rise to the occasion. They must express confidence in themselves, in their values, in their ability to live and to communicate with full serenity in Western societies. The revolution of trust we are calling for will depend first on self-confidence, on confidence in one's convictions: their task is to reappropriate their heritage and to develop toward it a positive yet critical intellectual attitude. They must be capable of affirming that the teachings of Islam summon Muslims first to spiritual life, to introspection, and to self-reform. They must forcefully insist that Muslims are expected to respect the laws of the countries in which they reside and to which they must be loyal. Millions of Muslims are, in fact, already proving every day that "religious integration" is an accomplished fact, that they are indeed at home in the Western countries whose tastes, culture, and psychology they have made their own.

Still, faced with legitimate fears, Muslim Westerners cannot simply minimize or avoid these questions. They must, as a matter of utmost urgency, develop a critical discourse that rejects the victim's stance, one that criticizes instead radical, literal, and/or cultural readings of the sources. In the name of the guiding principles of Islam, they must take a stand against, for instance, the use and misuse of their religion to justify terrorism, domestic violence, or forced marriage. The future of the Muslim spiritual community will necessarily require institutions of religious training (Islamic studies, Islamology, imam training schools, etc.) to be established in the West and help to respond to Western citizens' expectations. With the same critical attitude, they must learn to make distinctions; they must not endorse the confusion that surrounds the debates related to their societies: social problems, unemployment, marginalization, and immigration are not "religious problems" and have nothing to do with Islam as such. It is imperative to reject the "Islamization" of educational and socioeconomic issues that require political, not religious, solutions.

One of the most effective ways of responding to legitimate fears is to separate problems into their component parts but without disconnecting these closely related elements. "Deconstructing without disconnecting" means that we accept the obligation to distinguish what is strictly religious in nature from educational, social, or immigration-related issues, and then analyze how cause-and-effect relationships are established at the sociopolitical grass roots. Citizens of the Muslim faith must contribute to a reformulation of the political questions of the day. Seen in this light, unemployment, school failure, and delinquency have, as we already mentioned, no connection with Islam. Yet it is vitally necessary to grasp the reasons that Muslim citizens and residents bear the brunt of failure in these very areas. What new political, social, and city-planning policies can we propose to redress this state of affairs, new initiatives that would enable us to combat segregation and self-segregation, and encourage greater social justice and mixing at all levels of society?

Exploiting Fear

THE ARGUMENTS THAT WERE, YESTERDAY, the sole province of parties of the extreme right have unfortunately found a home within traditional mainstream parties. Political leaders increasingly play upon fear to mobilize voters and to promote increasingly hard-line policies for managing social problems, security, and immigration. At a loss for creative, innovative ideas for promoting cultural pluralism or for combating unemployment and social ghettoization, they prefer the dangerous rhetoric of protecting "identity" and "cultural homogeneity," of defending "Western values," of imposing strict limitations on "foreigners" with, of course, the whole apparatus of new security laws to fight terrorism. These political discourses play upon deep-seated apprehensions, perpetuate confusion over the terms of debate, and promote a binary approach to sociopolitical issues. The implicit terms of the debate are often reduced to a distinction between two entities: "We Westerners" and "They, the Muslims," even when citizens are Muslims and Westerners.

The constant return to the same questions in national political debates (violence, women, integration, etc.) is far from innocent; the question of "Islam" often becomes a diversionary tactic that political parties employ to undermine their adversaries and attract voters. Racist and xenophobic speech proliferates; the past is reinterpreted so as to exclude Islam from the slightest participation in the creation of the Western identity, henceforth redefined as purely Greco-Roman and Judeo-Christian; individuals are tested at the border to determine the "moral flexibility" of immigrants, and laws reinforcing security become reflexive in these times of fear and instability, not to mention the policies of intransigence whose ultimate effect is to criminalize immigrants and asylum seekers.

In response to these attempts at exploitation and, on occasion, to the manipulation that accompanies them, citizens of the Muslim religion must behave contrary to the natural reactions. Instead of withdrawing from the public debate and into isolation, they must make themselves heard; step out of their religious, social, cultural, or political ghettos; and move forward to meet and reassure their fellow citizens. The policies of those who exploit fear are intended to create precisely what they claim to combat: by perpetually accusing Muslims of not being integrated, of setting themselves apart, of setting up barriers between "them" and "us," and of shutting themselves up in a religious identity they view as exclusive, the intellectuals and politicians who warn against the "naivety" of other politicians, against "the Islamic threat" or the "failure" of pluralist society or of multiculturalism, spread suspicion, create divisions, and try to isolate the Muslims. As citizens, Muslims are today called upon to establish a rigorous critique of these very alarmist pronouncements that badly conceal the ideology they promote. In the name of Western values the Muslims must fight against policies that normalize common racism and discriminatory treatment, that stigmatize a portion of the population. The true loyal citizenship is a critical loyalty that means to refuse to have to permanently prove one's belonging to the society in full knowledge of one's responsibilities as a citizen, lay claim to one's rights, and carry out a thoroughgoing critique of government policies when these policies betray the ideals of a democratic society.

A New "We"

IF THERE IS A CONTRIBUTION that Muslim Westerners can bring to their respective societies, it is surely that of reconciliation. Confident in convictions, frank and rigorous in their critical outlook, armed with a broader understanding of Western societies, of their values, their history, and their aspirations, they are ideally placed to engage their fellow citizens in reconciling these societies with their own ideals. The vital issue today is not to compare social models or experiences in a fruitless debate (as we have witnessed among the United States, France, and Great Britain) but more simply, and in a far stricter and more demanding way, to take the measure of each society by comparing the ideals affirmed and proclaimed by its intellectuals and politicians with the concrete practices that can be observed at the social grass roots: human rights and equality of opportunity (between men and women, people of different origins, skin colors). We must bring constructive criticism to bear on our societies and measure words against deeds: all the citizens must adopt toward their society the same healthy self-critical attitude that Muslims must demonstrate toward their community.

Our societies are awaiting the emergence of a new "We." A "We" that would bring together men and women, citizens of all religions—and those without religion—who would undertake together to resolve the contradictions of their society: the right to work, to housing, to respect, against racism and all forms of discrimination, all offenses against human dignity. Such a "We" would henceforth represent this coming together of citizens confident in their values, defenders of pluralism in their common society, and respectful of the identities of others; citizens who seek to take up the challenge in the name of their shared values at the very heart of their societies. As loyal and critical citizens, as men and women of integrity, they join forces in a revolution of trust and confidence to stem the onrush of fear. Against shallow, emotional, even hysterical reactions they stand firm for rationality, for dialogue, for attentiveness, for a reasonable approach to complex social questions.

Local, National

THE FUTURE OF WESTERN SOCIETIES is now being played out at the local level. It is a matter of greatest urgency to set in motion national movements of local initiatives, in which women and men of different religions, cultures, and sensitivities can open new horizons of mutual understanding and shared commitment: horizons of trust. These shared projects must henceforth bring us together and give birth to a new "We" anchored in citizenship. Of course, "intercultural" and "interfaith" dialogues are both vital and necessary, but they cannot have the impact of the shared commitment of citizens in the priority fields: education, social divides, insecurity, racisms, discriminations, and more.

Together they must learn to question educational programs and to propose more inclusive approaches to the sum of remembered experiences that make up today's Western societies. These societies have changed, and the teaching of history must change apace; it must include the multiplicity of these experiences; it must even speak of the dark periods of history, those of which new citizens of the West have often been the original victims. Alongside the Enlightenment, and the progress and achievements of science and technology, something must also be said about slavery, about colonialism, about racism, genocide, and more. Objectively, without arrogance or a permanent sense of guilt. At the risk of touching off a competition for most-wounded victim status, a more objective reading of the memories building the current national history must be made official. On the social level, we must commit ourselves to a far more thoroughgoing social mixing in both our schools and our communities. Far more courageous and creative social and urban policies are needed, of course. But even now citizens can foster human interchange in and through projects focused on local democratic participation.

National political authorities must go along with, facilitate, and encourage such local dynamics.

Western societies will not win the battle against social insecurity, violence, and drugs through the sole security-based approach. What we need in our communities are social institutions, civic education, local job creation, and confidence-building policies. Local political authorities can do much to transform the prevailing atmosphere of suspicion, and citizens, including Muslims, must not hesitate to knock on their doors, to remind them that in a democratic society the elected representative is at the service of the voter, and not the opposite. It is imperative that we become involved in national affairs, that we not allow ourselves to be carried away by the passions generated on the international scene. Still, it is clear that a critical discussion of how immigration is managed has yet to take place in the West: it is no longer possible to strip the Third World of its riches and in the same breath treat those who flee poverty and dictatorial regimes as criminals. Not only is such behavior unjust and inhuman; it is intolerable. To be and to remain the voice of the voiceless of Iraq or Palestine, of Tibet or Chechnya, of abused women or of AIDS victims (particularly in Africa, even though medication exists) is to take a stand for reconciliation in the name of the ideals of dignity, human rights, and justice too often sacrificed on the altar of short-term political gain and geostrategic interests. In times of globalization, both local mutual trust and global critical mind pave the road toward reconciliation between civilizations.

A revolution of trust and confidence, of critical loyalty, the birth of a new "We" driven by national movements of local initiative: such are the contours of a responsible commitment by all the citizens in Western societies—for they lay claim to the benefits of a responsible, citizen-based ethic; for they want to promote the Western cultural richness; for they know that survival will depend, imperatively, upon a new sense of political creativity. Citizens must work in the long term, above and beyond the electoral deadlines that paralyze politicians and hinder the formulation of innovative, courageous policies. When the elected official has nowhere to turn, when he no longer can translate his ideas into reality, it falls to the voters, to the citizens, to lay full claim to their ideals, and to make them a reality.

Notes

1. See the text I have dedicated to him in Appendix I.
2. In the most advanced countries such as Britain, France, Belgium, the United States, or Canada. This phenomenon of definitive settlement, of passing from immigrant to citizen status, was to spread to all Western countries and continues to do so.
3. One translation for secularism in Arabic is *al-lâdiniyyah,* a system without religion.
4. An intelligent policy would be to involve long-standing Western Muslim citizens to help new migrants facing conscience or cultural conflict issues. Yet today, political discourse exploiting fear does exactly the opposite: it makes dangerous use of new migrants' difficulties and of some shocking stories—to cast suspicion over all Muslims, whether citizens or new immigrants.
5. This is not always so: some converts, instead of taking advantage of their knowledge of society, adopt a position of self-marginalization and self-segregation, thus becoming strangers in their own society.
6. *To Be a European Muslim* (Leicester, UK: The Islamic Foundation, 1998); *Western Muslims and the Future of Islam* (New York: Oxford University Press, 2004).
7. This is what I explained and analyzed in the book *To Be a European Muslim* when I spoke of a Muslim identity that is always open, always inclusive, always on the move.
8. Belonging to the "ummah," to the spiritual community or "faith community," is subject to the same conditions mentioned above. As I noted in *To Be a European Muslim*, it is a matter of respecting principles and contracts: thus, Muslims are strictly bound by the laws of the countries in which they live in the West, and they must moreover be critical and self-critical toward their fellow believers (as indeed toward all men

and all societies). If those latter uphold justice, they must support them; if they do not, they must resist them. Muslims belong to a "spiritual community" based on principles, and if the community or its members betray those principles, their duty is to stop them or oppose them. The Prophet of Islam once said: "Help your brother, whether he is just or unjust!" His companions inevitably questioned him about the support they were to give an unjust brother: how could that be? And the Prophet answered, reversing the perspective: "Prevent him [the unjust brother] from performing injustice; this is how you will support him!" (*hadîth* reported by al-Bukhârî).

9. On the level of more learned, specialized terminology, this reformism defines itself as *salafî*, meaning that its advocates want to return to the faithfulness of the first generations of Muslims (the *salaf*) and recapture the energy, creativity, and boldness of early scholars who did not hesitate to suggest new approaches to new contexts. This word can be confusing because it is used with another, opposed meaning. There are literalist *salafî* trends that also refer to the *salaf* to advocate a return to rigid, literal interpretations of the past. For the former group, faithfulness involves movement (since times and societies have changed) while for the latter it implies freezing the text beyond time and environment.

10. This is the subject of my book *Radical Reform: Islamic Ethics and Liberation* (New York: Oxford University Press, 2009), which deals with this imperative evolution of contemporary Muslim thinking.

11. I have, for instance, taken a position in Canada (and in Britain after the Archbishop of Canterbury's remarks) in debates over the religious arbitration and conciliation courts granted to and used by other religions. A polemic appeared when some Muslims asked to be granted the same rights as other religions. From a strictly legal standpoint, the Muslim organizations which demanded such equality were right, but my position was that in fact Muslims did not need those internal adjustments and that solutions could be found within the existing legal framework.

12. I have explained in many books and articles that my position is to encourage Muslim citizens to enroll their children in the public school system where they will learn to live with their fellow citizens of various origins and cultures. Private schools, which anyway only receive 2 percent or 3 percent of Muslim children, are neither a panacea nor a future-oriented choice. Engaging in the state school system, as parents and as students, is a necessity. It remains that the system should be reformed in depth, for the mixing of social statuses and cultures is but an illusion in what ought to be common, equal schooling for all. Some

state schools are actually social and cultural ghettos, and inequalities in treatment within the public system are simply unacceptable. If nothing is done in this field, it can be no surprise that some people think of creating efficient alternative structures exclusively for Muslims: anyway, such segregation already exists in state schools in some areas or suburbs (where 80 percent or 90 percent of pupils are "of immigrant origin" or "Muslims"), with the additional bitter truth that achievement levels in those schools are very low and offer children no hope of success.

13. As Muslim jurists (*fuqahâ*) have defined it according to their specialty as scholars of Islamic law and jurisprudence (*fiqh*).

14. See my books *To Be a European Muslim, Western Muslims and the Future of Islam*, and especially *Radical Reform: Islamic Ethics and Liberation*, in which I put forward a new categorization of the ethical finalities in Islam's message.

15. See on my website (www.tariqramadan.com) the information about this European campaign "Joining hands against forced marriages" in collaboration with the Rotterdam municipality and the "think tank" I chair, The European Muslim Network.

16. See the reports published so far: *Report on City Tour of Tariq Ramadan March 2007–June 2007*, Municipality of Rotterdam, Youth, Education and Society (Jeugd, Onderwijs en Samenleving), September 2007, and *Citizenship, Identity and A Sense of Belonging: Bridge of Trust, Education: The First Pillar*, Municipality of Rotterdam, Youth, Education and Society (Jeugd, Onderwijs en Samenleving), April 2008.

17. An academic component is linked to this project, with the creation of a "Citizenship and Identity" chair at the University of Rotterdam. Three PhD projects have started over comparative studies of local policies and dynamics. See my webpage at the university: www.eur.nl/fsw/staff/homepages/ramadan.

18. In Switzerland, some leaders of the far right party Union Démocratique du Centre (UDC) have demanded that I be stripped of my nationality because my commitment for Islam was evidence of my failure to integrate. They moreover demanded that building minarets be prohibited for they symbolized Muslims' settlement and the "arrogance of their colonization" contradicting the "Christian essence" of Swiss culture.

19. But who was also, it is generally overlooked, a Muslim judge (*qâdî*) as well as a fervent worshiper.

20. This is what the philosopher and medievalist Alain de Libera has been doing in book after book: see in particular his seminal *Penser au Moyen Âge*.

21. See my book *Radical Reform: Islamic Ethics and Liberation*.

22. This was a pun as I argued for the need "to foresee the four Cs."

23. *"The Quest for Meaning, a Philosophy of Pluralism."*

24. One must also denounce the hypocrisy of Arab states, which after all bear the main responsibility for letting down the Palestinians and for their current disarray.

25. That is the idea underlying the *Charter for Compassion* initiated by Karen Armstrong, which develops that idea that the realm of the heart is necessary to the finality of justice. The Group of Sages, to which I belong, met in February 2009 in Geneva to finalize the terms of the Charter, about which the public has been invited to write and react.

26. That is the title of my latest book: *The Quest for Meaning, a Philosophy of Pluralism*.

27. The project was precisely entitled *Giving Europe a Soul*.

28. This is what I have called the three "Ls," which Muslim citizens have now acquired: mastering the national *language*, respecting the *law*, and (even) maintaining critical *loyalty* to their society.

29. Including those mentioned earlier intended to test their loyalty, of the type: who are you primarily?

30. To the notable and paradoxical exception of language acquisition: it seems that the nature of requirements as to mastering the language (on the job market) is higher even as the young are becoming aware of the difficulties that are awaiting them in finding work. The combined phenomena of high requirements and disaffection would, the report goes, seem to explain this regression, which nevertheless is not confirmed in all countries. The report is in Dutch and is soon to be published in English (wholly or in part).

31. See Appendix II: Manifesto for a New "We."

32. One should also mention here the writings of the new "terrorism experts," who keep fostering suspicion and feeding rumors about possible connections, without ever providing evidence of their hypothetical conclusions. That enables them to go on giving "expert opinions" about "terrorist networks" and thereby earning some money.

33. A prominent institution as far as the memory and principles of French secularism are concerned.

34. The term "Judeo-Christian" is a recent one. It would have been impossible to put it this way during the Second World War. This is an a posteriori ideological reconstruction.

35. See the website www.palestineglobalresistance.info that sets forth the movement's philosophy and the characteristics of the synergies that should be established.

36. This is what John J. Mearsheimer and Stephen M. Walt have shown in a recent study: *The Israel Lobby and US Foreign Policy* (New York: Farrar, Straus and Giroux, 2007).

37. After I waited for two years and initiated a lawsuit to find out the reason my visa had been revoked, the Department of Homeland Security claimed that I had given money to a Palestinian organization while I "should reasonably have known" that this organization "had links with the terrorist movement Hamas." Yet, not only is this organization not blacklisted—to this day—anywhere in Europe (where I live), but I gave about 700 euros to this organization between 1998 and 2002, a year before it was blacklisted in the United States. Thus I "should reasonably have known" a year before the Department of Homeland Security itself that it was going to be suspected! This is all the more ludicrous when one learns that such ridiculous and arbitrary decisions are retroactive! It should be added that 80 percent of the questions I had to answer during my two interviews at the U.S. embassy in Switzerland were about my positions over the war in Iraq and the Palestinian resistance. I repeated that such resistance is legitimate even though I disagree with the means used (killing innocents cannot be justified).

38. Concurring evidence shows that the American intervention in Afghanistan had already been planned before the September 11, 2001, terrorist attacks.

39. It must be stressed here that some supposedly "liberal" Muslims have no qualms about supporting dictators: being religious "liberals" does not mean being political "democrats." The Western public is often misled over this issue: for instance, many Tunisian intellectuals claim to be liberals as far as religion is concerned but they side with dictatorship concerning politics. Examples abound.

40. Their having an "exotic" name is not enough: those persons may very well still belong to the same "universe of reference."

Index